SOCIAL RELATIONS IN A
SECONDARY SCHOOL

SOCIAL RELATIONS
IN A
SECONDARY SCHOOL

by

DAVID H. HARGREAVES

LONDON AND HENLEY
ROUTLEDGE & KEGAN PAUL
NEW JERSEY : HUMANITIES PRESS

First published 1967
by Routledge & Kegan Paul Limited
39 Store Street
London WC1E 7DD and
Broadway House, Newtown Road
Henley-on-Thames, Oxon RG9 1EN

Printed in Great Britain by
Lowe & Brydone Printers Limited
Thetford, Norfolk

© David H. Hargreaves 1967

Reprinted 1968, 1970, 1973 and 1976

ISBN 0 7100 6868 9 (p)
ISBN 0 7100 3476 8 (c)

CONTENTS

PREFACE

The research on which this book is based was part of a project conducted by the Department of Social Anthropology and Sociology of the University of Manchester and financed by the Ministry of Education (now the Department of Education and Science). The aim of the project was to provide an analysis of the school as a dynamic system of social relations through an intensive study of interaction processes and day-to-day behaviour within the school. This book is the result of an intensive study of a Secondary Modern School for Boys in a town in the North of England.

I am very grateful to the Chief Education Officer and to the Education Committee of the town in which 'Lumley' School is situated for permission to undertake research in one of their schools, and to various Local Government Officials who willingly gave up their time to provide me with valuable information.

My thanks are also due to many friends and colleagues for encouragement and criticism, especially to Professor Peter M. Worsley, Dr. Valdo G. Pons, Mrs. Audrey Lambart, Dr. Harold Entwistle and Mr. Eric Hoyle. Mr. R. Mohan Mankikar constructed the sociometric charts and gave me considerable assistance with the analysis of data, as did my brother, Mr. Philip Hargreaves, Mrs. D. Shelton and Miss Barbara Kasinska.

Most of all I owe a deep debt of gratitude to the Headmaster, teachers and boys of Lumley School. They were under no obligation to assist me, yet they gave generously of their time, knowledge and experience. At no stage did anyone complain of the many demands I made upon them. The fact that they welcomed an outside researcher so warmly into the school and that they co-operated so fully and so patiently in the research is an outstanding testimony to the concern of such teachers to accept the challenge of educating the children in their care. I can but hope that in some small way this research will contribute to an alleviation and to a wider understanding of their many problems.

DAVID H. HARGREAVES

Manchester, July 1966.

INTRODUCTION

This book is written at a time when the whole English Educational System is subject to reorganization and change. A study of a Secondary Modern School may thus seem inappropriate at a point when most Local Authorities are preparing or implementing schemes for the reorganization of their schools along comprehensive lines. Yet the social system of the school includes many basic social processes which may be independent of, or little affected by, comprehensive reorganization, and it is to some of these basic processes that this study is devoted.

The Newsom Report has revitalized our interest in children of average and below average ability and has drawn our attention to the schools in 'problem areas' – some twenty per cent of all Secondary Modern Schools – where social and educational problems loom most terrifyingly. Many teachers in these schools received the news that the school leaving age will be raised from fifteen to sixteen years with alarm and dismay; they already feel overwhelmed with apparently insoluble problems. Yet they are problems which demand solutions, for the sake of both teachers and pupils. Lumley Secondary Modern School for Boys is situated in one of these 'problem areas'.

The writer spent a complete year at the school. For the first two terms he was present for the whole school day. He taught all the fourth year boys at some stage, as well as other year-groups; he observed the pupils in lessons conducted by all the teachers; he administered questionnaires and conducted interviews; he used every available opportunity for informal discussion with the boys; he accompanied them on some official school visits and holidays; he joined them in some of their out-of-school activities. In a word, the researcher entered the school as a participant-observer, armed with his own training and teaching experience and with the intention of examining the behaviour and attitudes of boys in school and their relationships with the teachers and with one another.

The study is thus social psychological and micro-sociological in orientation. Many limitations restrict the scope of the study. Differences in individual psychology, such as personality factors, have been excluded, and many sociological variables receive scant attention. The study does not intend to test specific hypotheses derived from current theories. Rather, the research is exploratory in nature and focuses broadly on the structure of the informal groups of pupils and the influence of such groups on the educative process. At the same time an attempt has been made to find ways in which these observed processes can be measured and subjected to statistical analysis. Such a relatively unstructured research procedure is fraught with difficulties and dangers, some of which are outlined in Appendix I. To what extent the work has produced useful results and insights can be judged only from further research. The content of this initial exploratory investigation is far from complete, but it is hoped that some of the pieces of the jigsaw puzzle have been put together in a way which will prove useful, but which does not do too much injustice to the whole picture.

It is difficult to describe human behaviour without appearing to make judgements on the actors involved. When man writes about man his terms seem very subjective and value-loaded. Although this analysis of Lumley School has been written as objectively as possible, it may often appear that the writer is emphasizing the defects of the school at the expense of its virtues. The aim of the study is to describe the structure and unintended consequences of selected aspects of human behaviour and organization in the school. It is through the examination of the conflicts and deleterious effects of human action and school organization that our understanding of the social system of the school can be advanced. But this is not to disparage or impugn the sincerity and industry of many of the teachers. The primary function of the social researcher is to make a diagnosis, not prescribe a cure.

The work would be a more adequate contribution to our knowledge if all the boys in the school had been studied. Since such a task was beyond the powers of one man, the study is largely restricted to fourth year boys, aged between fourteen and fifteen years, who were mostly in their final year at school. The assumption is that these fourth year boys represent a crystallization of the values inculcated by the school and an end-product of the educative process.

Wherever possible the boys speak for themselves. The quotations from the boys are not reconstructions from memory, but the actual words spoken by boys from tape recordings of discussions made only after the writer had developed a relationship of mutual trust with the pupils. To what extent the presence of the tape recorder caused the boys to distort their expressed attitudes and opinions is difficult to judge; but it must be said that the presence or absence of the microphone seemed for the most part to have little effect on the content or progress of the discussion. Of course, all the quotations cannot be taken at their face value; nor does the writer endorse all the opinions. The extensive use made of this recorded material may be justified on the grounds that such evidence is more direct, vivid and self-evident in its implications than the narration of observed incidents.

There is a sense in which this work may be regarded as a study of the streaming system in one school. This was not the aim of the research. It is simply that the structure of social relations in the school is to a large extent moulded by the streaming system. To treat this study as a general evaluation of the social consequences of streaming would be entirely unwarranted.

The social system of the school is a unity which cannot easily be broken into segments. Each chapter represents an analysis of one aspect which is inextricably bound up with all the others, and is thus an artificial selection of material focusing on one particular area. Not until the end of the book are the various segments brought together to form a more complete picture.

Chapter One describes the location and organization of the school and sets the scene for the chapters that follow. In Chapter Two the social structure of each of the fourth year forms is described. We examine the groups of friends, the status or power hierarchy of the form and the prevailing norms or standards of behaviour. It becomes clear that the four forms are highly differentiated from one another in many respects. The important individual boys are named, since they reappear in later chapters. After a chapter on measurements of what has been observed, there follows a discussion of the relations between the streams in Chapter Four. The next chapter analyses the relations between the teachers and pupils and the differences between streams in the conception of the teacher-pupil relationship. The ways in which teachers are allocated to streams, perceive and treat the pupils, and adapt to their teaching situations are assessed.

Chapter Six returns to the boys themselves and discusses their delinquent activities. In particular, the growth, structure and behaviour of the low stream 'delinquent group' is described and the conflict of these boys with the teachers is illustrated. Chapter Seven presents some data on the boys' homes, parental attitudes and out-of-school activities.

In Chapter Eight the previous discussion is drawn together in the form of a 'model' of the social system of the school. The existence of two opposing subcultures is posited and the process by which they develop is discussed in terms of the values of our society, the home environment of the boys, the organization of the school and the power of the segregated streams to inculcate attitudes and impose patterns of behaviour on their members. The unintended and unrecognized effects of the structure of social relations and school organization are examined. The final chapter attempts to estimate some of the conclusions which may be derived from the research and to formulate some implications for the organization of the school.

Chapter One

LUMLEY SECONDARY MODERN SCHOOL

Lumley is a district or ward in a highly industrialized and densely populated town in the North of England. Within this population the unskilled manual workers are over-represented and the professional occupations are under-represented in comparison with the national averages. Many of the professional people who work in the town live outside the town boundaries in residential areas within easy reach of the central sections of the town. Although the town council has provided a number of fine parks and is attempting to beautify the town with modern buildings, there remain large areas consisting of closely packed streets of small terraced houses with four or five rooms, built in the later nineteenth century period of industrial expansion. From the outside many of these houses reveal the care and pride that their owners lavish upon them; inside, the atmosphere is warm and friendly. But to the visitor a sense of dirt, dreariness and sometimes squalor prevails.

Most of the houses in Lumley ward are of the small terraced variety, though a few, especially around the tiny park that forms its centre, are of a rather larger and grander design. Lumley is rather like a small island, surrounded on two sides by the tentacles of industry and on the third by a main road, which is lined with shops and stores. These natural boundaries enclose the maze of stereotyped streets, most of which have 'corner shops' or general stores, existing in the age of supermarkets on offers of credit and a localized clientele. Public houses are profuse, but like the numerous workshops, merge into their background unnoticed. The smoke and the grime give an air of sorrowful dilapidation to the larger buildings of churches and schools. For much of the year this little world seems grey and dismal, but on sunny days women and old people sit at the front door, on the step or a chair, and call to one another across the street, above the noise of countless small children who play undisturbed.[1]

Lumley is scheduled for redevelopment. On the fringes the old houses have been replaced by Council flats. Of those whose homes are demolished, some 25 per cent opt for a new Council house in an overspill area outside the town. The rest accept a flat or a vacant house in Lumley.

Lumley Secondary Modern School for Boys was built as part of the Council's policy of redeveloping the town's secondary schools. It is less than a decade old, but the building and amenities show few signs of lavish spending. It has no playing fields of its own, and the single playground is small and without a shelter against bad weather conditions. Initially it was a mixed school, but a few years later when the girls' school was completed, it restricted its intake to boys. The pupils are drawn almost exclusively from Lumley: before the erection of the two Modern Schools they had attended the all-age schools which then became purely primary. The school originally contained some six hundred children, but demolition of homes and consequent migrant population has caused this to fall slowly and steadily to around four hundred and fifty boys, taught by a staff of twenty-six teachers.

In Lumley School the pupils are streamed by ability and achievement. On entry, they are not specially assessed for allocation to streams. The Headmaster assigns boys to the five streams on the basis of their scores in the eleven-plus examination. Where two boys with the same eleven-plus score fall at a point of division between two streams, the boy with the more favourable Primary school report is assigned to the higher stream. The school is 'fed' by six main Primary schools, all of which are in the immediate vicinity of the school, and the new entrants are divided into five streams, A to E, the lowest (E) stream containing boys who are considered backward or retarded. Each form thus contains boys from each of the Primary schools and investigation showed that there is no evidence of any association between particular streams and particular Primary schools.

This study concentrates on the fourth year pupils, some hundred boys divided into five streams, 4A to 4E, most of whom leave during the course of this final year. Half of them reach the statutory leaving age during the year and are allowed to leave school at the end of the Easter Term. The rest may leave at the end of the Summer Term. The research was based upon these fourth year boys since it was felt that they would be more articulate in their verbal and written expressions of their views than more junior boys; they would more easily form friendly relationships with the researcher; they would more fully embody the influences of the school and the peer-group. The pupils of 4E were excluded from special study, not only because of their severe difficulties in answering questionnaires without individual attention, but also because they tended to form a separate group in terms of friendship choices and the special teachers assigned to them.[2]

Stream changes at Lumley can occur at any stage of a boy's career. Examinations are held at the end of each of the three terms in each academic year. The boys occupying the two or three positions at the top and bottom of each form are open to promotion or demotion to other adjacent streams, according to the recommendations of the form teacher and subject to the final decision of the Headmaster. During the four years which a boy spends at Lumley school, it is quite possible for him to change streams several times. One of the boys in the present 4A began his career in the school in 1E, but such cases of movement from one extreme to the other are exceptional. It is more common for a boy to move one or two streams up or down; it is not unusual for a boy to move up or down one stream and then return to his original stream. In September 1964 the average number of stream changes per boy was calculated for pupils in the fourth year. As this figure is very slightly less than one change in the previous three years, it is clear the average number of stream changes per boy is comparatively low. This is verified by the fact that 41 per cent of these boys have never changed streams at all by the fourth year. If we consider each stream separately, this figure varies between 30 per cent and 50 per cent. That the boys in the A and the E streams should change less frequently is understandable since movement from these forms can take place in only one direction: the boys in the A stream cannot move up and the boys in the E stream cannot move down.

In the latter part of the academic year 1963/4 the Headmaster of Lumley Secondary Modern School received advice from the

Local Education Authority concerning the introduction of the Certificate of Secondary Education (C.S.E.) into the Secondary Schools under its control. This examination would be available to pupils who were willing to stay on for a fifth year, which for the Secondary Modern Schools signified an additional year at school beyond the statutory leaving age of fifteen years. Since the proportion of children in the town already remaining at school for a fifth year is well below the national average, the Authority was anxious to encourage teachers and pupils in the Modern Schools to avail themselves of this new opportunity to enter candidates for a nationally recognized examination, and to prepare pupils for the raising of the school leaving age to sixteen years.

The advent of the C.S.E. was received with mixed feelings by the staff at Lumley. Some of the teachers regarded this examination as a stimulating opportunity to provide the more able pupils with an incentive to greater academic achievement and a Certificate comparable with the G.C.E. Others, however, believed that no useful purpose would be served by encouraging boys to spend an additional year at school, since only a small minority would be capable of obtaining good results, and a poor Certificate would hinder rather than assist their career prospects.[3] The Headmaster assembled all the boys from the third year and explained to them the nature and purpose of the C.S.E. Each boy was given an explanatory letter to take home to his parents, with the request that those parents who provisionally wished their sons to enter for this examination should indicate their intentions to the School.

The Headmaster decided that the fourth year would be streamed in relation to the prospective candidates for the C.S.E. During the following academic year, the A stream in the fourth year would consist of those boys who intended to remain at school for a fifth year and take the C.S.E. 4B would comprise those of the more able boys who intended to leave at Easter or Summer of the fourth year. The rest of the fourth year would be streamed according to the usual academic requirements i.e. achievement in tests given at the end of the third year. 4A and 4B, and possibly a few of 4C, would take the local Leaving Certificate at the end of the fourth year as usual.

As the pupils and their parents had been warned that entry to the C.S.E. course would necessitate a combination of native ability and conscientious hard work during the fourth year, it is hardly surprising that those expressing a desire to take this course should come predominantly from the A stream, now in their third year at school. Few boys were certain of their intentions; most intended to use the results of the Local Leaving Certificate Examination and their school reports as indicators of their progress and thus of their possible success for the C.S.E.

The fourth year forms of the period under investigation, the academic year 1964/5, were thus organized as follows. 4A consisted of the thirteen 3A boys, with the five boys from 3B and the four boys from 3C, all of whom intended to take the C.S.E. The numbers in 4A were made up to thirty with the eight boys in the highest academic positions. Of the boys in 3A who did not wish to remain at school for a fifth year, the seven boys occupying the lowest academic positions in the summer examinations at the end of the third year were removed into 4B. Four boys from 3C were transferred to 4D and replaced by three 3D boys.

Our interest now moves from the *formal* organization of the fourth year streams to the *informal* processes at work in each stream, that is, those processes which are not formulated officially by the school. It is to this problem of examining differences between streams in informal organization that the next chapter is devoted.

Chapter Two

THE FOURTH YEAR
FORMS

We have seen that the formal organization of the school divides each year into five units by the streaming system. Boys in any one form are thus united for administrative purposes under one form-teacher and for teaching purposes with a variety of teachers. For the major part of the school day, members of each form are taught as a separate group. Each form can be regarded as a 'sub-group' of all the boys in any one year. Members of any one form have greater opportunity for meeting one another, making mutual assessments and developing friendships. Because members of each form have differential opportunities for interaction, we would expect that friendships would be more likely to occur between members of the same form than between members of different forms. At the end of the Autumn Term 1964, when these fourth year boys had been in their new forms for three months, they were asked to make a list of the boys that they 'went around with' most in school (Q.1).* This 'sociometric' technique for investigating the informal processes of groups was originally devised by Moreno,[1] and has been used extensively by researchers. Moreno stipulated that 'sociometric' questions should be 'real' ones in the sense that they should refer to some future change. The most common question is thus, 'With whom would you like to sit next term?' and the children must understand that their choices will be effected the following term. Such a question can provide useful insights into the informal structure of a group, but the question asks for *preferred* friends, not for *actual* friends. We are more interested in which boys an individual actually interacts with, not in those with whom he might like to interact. The results to the question are given in Table 1. It can be seen

* For the full list of questionnaire items, *see* Appendix III.

6

that the friendship choices are highly stream-bound. In each form over half the boys selected as friends come from the same form. Of those choices which are made from other streams, the majority are directed to adjacent streams. Only in exceptional circumstances do friendship choices extend beyond one stream from the form of origin. This stream-specificity of choices indicates that we may indeed be justified in regarding each stream as a sub-group of the fourth year as a whole, and that members of any one stream interact with one another more frequently than they do with members of other streams.

Much of social psychological work has been concerned with the analysis of the process of interaction. We have been furnished with a set of concepts in which analysis may be formulated. This is not a case of introducing 'jargon' for its own sake, or even for the sake of making it sound 'scientific'. These concepts are tools with which the living, complex, *dynamic* processes of interaction can be summarized and inter-related.

TABLE I

Friendship choices—'go around with'

| | Form | RECIPIENT | | | | | | | |
		4A	4B	4C	4D	4E	Others	N	Mean choices per boy
DONOR	4A	78	12	2	0	2	7	113	3·8
	4B	11	77	6	1	0	5	99	3·5
	4C	2	7	70	17	1	2	83	3·6
	4D	1	1	23	60	8	7	75	3·4

Figures are percentages.

Interactions are never random. Even when two strangers meet for the first time, what they say conforms to a *pattern*. They will probably begin with a few conventional remarks on which agreement is certain – in England this will be the current weather! – and progress by a process of mutually exploratory remarks to

7

a deeper relationship or to a rapid termination of the interaction. Small groups who interact regularly and frequently reveal patterns in their behaviour. Usually the members are conscious of who is 'in' the group and who is not, and those who are 'in' can be differentiated from those who are 'out'. Among those who are in the group we can observe similarities between members, both in their behaviour and the communications they make to one another. If the group is one of friends, the members will like one another and will *expect* certain things from their fellow-members. This is so not only because they know each other well and can therefore predict within limits what another member will do or say, but also because a person's membership of the group indicates that he behaves in ways which are acceptable to other members. In a word, groups exhibit *norms*. By norm, we mean that which defines the behaviour which is expected or desired by the group as a whole. We may regard these norms as the behavioural expression of the *values* of the group. Norms, of course, cover various aspects of behaviour, some of which may be relevant and some of which may be irrelevant to the group. For example, one's religious beliefs may be irrelevant to membership of a cricket team, but they will be relevant to membership of a Church organization. Groups, then, are united by certain common values and produce norms which define the criteria of membership and the expected forms of behaviour.

Norms influence people in many ways. They contribute to a member's sense of identity and they control or regulate the behaviour of the group. Members will differ in the extent to which they *conform to* or *deviate from* the norms. Those who conform will clearly be more acceptable to other members than those who deviate; the latter, if they deviate too sharply, will be rejected by the group. The important part is that the group will constantly exert pressure on members to conform to its central norms. To deviate is to invite punishment or rejection. When the norms are weak, the group will have less control over its members; if they weaken further, the group will tend to disperse. When the norms are more clearly defined, the group will have much greater control over its members.

Members of groups are rarely equivalent: they vary in the length of their membership, the esteem in which other members hold them, the contribution they make to achieving the group's goals, the extent of their conformity to the group's norms. In other words, members of groups are differentiated into a hierarchy, by which members are differentiated according to the prestige the other members confer on them. By the term 'leaders', ambiguous though it is, we often refer to those persons who are for various reasons held in the highest esteem. In this study we shall refer to this structure as the *informal status hierarchy*. Those with high prestige in the group, its 'leaders', will have high informal status; those with low prestige will have low informal status. The way in which prestige is acquired depends on the type and activity and composition of the group, as well as its norms, but we can safely say that there is tendency for those with high informal status to conform more than the others to the group's norms,[2] and for those with low informal status to be non-conformists or deviants from the group's norms.

In our analysis of Lumley School we are concerned with the fourth year boys, which may be said to form a group, since membership of the fourth year is clearly defined for all. This fourth year is divided into forms. Each form is divided into sub-groups of particular friends. These friendship groups will be referred to as *cliques*. Our analysis of the fourth year thus requires us to divide the hundred boys into forms, and then each form into its respective cliques. Because members of any one form interact more frequently with one another than with members of other forms, and because the friendship choices are concentrated in the form of the choice-donor, we may expect norms to develop within each form. By studying the content of the norms, the processes of conformity and deviation, and the development of informal status hierarchies, we will be able to specify the distinctive qualities of each of the fourth year forms. And part of the analysis will concern the differences between cliques within any one form. Indeed, it is through the clique differences among members of the same form, that the norm differences will be clarified.

Before we examine the norms in each of the fourth year forms, we must consider three measures which will be used to aid the analysis. The first is the 'friendship' question given to each boy. The results are drawn in several charts, in which boys are represented by circles around numbers, and choices by linking lines. The second is an attempt to measure the informal status of each boy in his own form. Each boy was asked to score every other boy in his form in terms of his 'leadership' (Q.7) and from these scores each boy was assigned a rank.[3] Each boy can thus be ranked for his position on the informal status hierarchy in the same way that he is ranked by the teachers for his academic performance in examinations. The reader should note that the informal status technique attempts to measure power and influence rather than personal preference or popularity.[4] Popularity and power are rather different dimensions, even though they are frequently associated. In this analysis we are less interested in the extent to which a boy is liked than in his power to exert influence over others. If we can detect those boys with the greatest social power, we should be able to specify the norms which dominate in each form. These two measures are derived from questionnaires given to the boys at the end of the Autumn Term 1964. The third measure, academic status, is based on the examination results of the same period.

We must now relate our concepts to the informal organization in each form in the hope of producing a more refined and incisive analysis than is possible in a less technical description.

FORM 4A

Most of these boys, as we have seen, intended to stay on for a fifth year at school in order to sit for the C.S.E. examination. 23 of the boys came from 3A, 5 from 3B and 4 from 3C. The result of the 'friendship' question which asked for the names of the boys in the whole school with whom they associated most frequently are given in Chart 1. Three major cliques are in evidence by this stage, and observation did not reveal any major changes during the rest of the academic year.[5]

The form as a whole is dominated by Clique A, which, though possessing links to many other boys, has six main members. Its dominance is clear from its informal status rank average of 5·5 which is a measure of the high 'social power' of this group. The accepted leader of the group was 29 (Adrian),* who was informal status rank 1, and School Captain. Three of the other members

* Boys who are mentioned frequently are given names as well as numbers. The initial letter is the same as the boy's form: Thus *A*drian comes from 4A, Brian from 4B and so on.

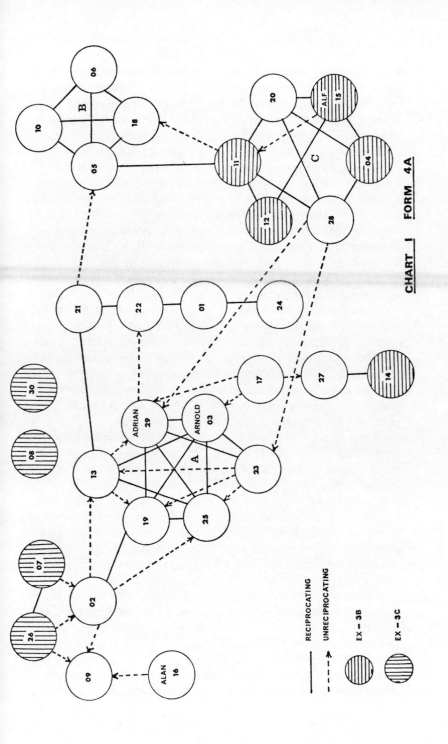

RECIPROCATING

UNRECIPROCATING

EX — 3B

EX — 3C

CHART I   FORM 4A

were appointed prefects. The group was academically superior, the average form position for the group in the Christmas examinations being 10·2. Four of the boys played for the school First Team in rugby or football. Adrian played for the town's schoolboy team. This group was also very popular with the teachers.

Clique B is a small but intimate group: all the friendship choices are reciprocated. The average informal status rank is 10·7, lower than for the A clique but well above average. Its academic average, 4·2, indicates that it is the 'intellectual' group of the form. From observation of classroom behaviour, we can detect that it divides into two mutual friendships, 05 and 10, 06 and 18. These two pairs would sit together during those lessons when the group as a whole could not sit together. Only one of the boys took a strong interest in sport, being a member of a First Team, and two of the members were prefects.

Clique C is linked to Clique B by 11, who reciprocates a choice with 05 and offers an unreciprocated choice to 18. The group consists in the main of 'newcomers' to the A stream. Their informal status rank average is 18·7, which is lower than that of the two other major cliques, as is their academic average of 19·5. Four of the boys were active sportsmen and two were prefects as well. A third was one of the school's most able gymnasts. Two of these boys possessed considerable ability at Art.

Of the four *isolates*, that is those boys who receive no friendship choices, two come from 3C. The remaining two ex-3C boys are chosen by each other. Of the two ex-3A boys who are isolates, 16 was a Scot who had but recently joined the school. Clique A is dominant not only in terms of its high informal status rank average, but also its centrality in friendship choices. Almost every boy in the form is linked, either directly or indirectly, to this clique. In other words, not only is this A clique powerful in the influence it can exert, but it is popular in that its members are sought as friends.

Further light is thrown on the form structure by the results of the question which asked the boys to indicate those form members whom they *dis*liked (Q.2). The most rejected member is the newcomer 15 from the C clique, who is named by ten boys, six of whom come from the A clique or their 'satellites'. 16, the isolate Scot, is rejected seven times. As we shall see, these boys who are rejected are those who deviate most sharply from the norms imposed by the A clique, and it is significant that the four rejections of Adrian come from boys who were not formerly in 3A.

Such a discussion may appear to be somewhat tiresome to the reader. Constant reference to Chart 1 and the use of numbers rather than names tends to drain the picture of the form of its natural colour. The representation of the dynamic system of relationships among thirty boys, in all its kaleidoscopic variety, can be most vividly communicated only in a film or a novel. Yet this dry systematization of their relationships is a necessary prerequisite to our understanding of the structure and 'culture' of the form.

The division of the A/B streams in the fourth year according to the pupils' intentions with regard to the C.S.E. tended to exaggerate and enhance the apparent academic superiority of the A stream. The A stream tended to be conscious of itself as maintaining an academic leadership, a view which was fostered by the teachers. But their loss of those boys who did not intend to take the C.S.E. and the developing sense of 'We are leaving' in the B stream contributed to 4A's awareness of academic responsibilities beyond the normal range. The novelty of potentially becoming the first fifth year form had its effects on the image of the form in its members' eyes. In part staff pressures and expectations of this potential first C.S.E. group were responsible.

Mr. ——— won't let us help with the Christmas decorations or anything like that. Not if we're missing a lesson.

If you're on milk duty, Mr. ——— won't let you out to do it. He makes you get someone out of a lower form to do it, 'cos you're not supposed to be missing a lesson.

Me and him once went in Mr. ———'s lesson selling poppies and it were P.E., you know; we was missing P.E. and he told us off, telling us about not training for the football team and that.

The boys expressed their concern for academic achievement in their impatience with those subjects which they did not intend to take in the C.S.E. Religious Education and Music in particular were the subject of criticism and ridicule. Even in main subjects, they did not take life easily, but were concerned to get the most out of their lessons. When they thought the lessons inadequate in some way, the teachers were criticized.

> In the morning he says, 'When you come this afternoon we'll have a spelling test.' But when you come he lets you go into the library to read and forgets all about it and we've been learning these hard spelling words. Why does he have to waste time like that?

> In Art you have two teachers, Mr. ——— and Mr. ———. They're teaching different things. Mr. ——— is teaching you that you should only draw what you can see and Mr. ——— wants you to draw from your imagination. You don't know where you are. They had a big argument in class the other day.

> They should take some periods of English and give them to Science.

This stress of the dominating high-status members on academic achievement had its effects on their relations with the newcomers into the A stream. The general feeling of most of the ex-3A boys at the end of their first term in 4A was summed up as follows.

> 4A's not as good as 3A.

> There are sort of two groups. One that's come up from 3A and then the others.

The obvious implication is that the ex-3A boys resented the loss of seven of their members from the A stream. This, however, does not appear to be the case. Only two of these seven 3A boys, who went into 4B were given favourable comments by the leading 4A boys. Typical would be:

> I'm glad ———'s gone. He used to be my friend. He's mad now. He's always saying stupid things.

> The people that have come up are better than them as went in 4B.

If the newcomers were seen as in many ways preferable to the former 3A boys, why should they be resented? The explanation for the rejection of the newcomers seems to lie not in the resentment against the loss of particular individuals, nor in the acquisition of particular individuals. As we shall see later, 3A had been a very happy form, which their form-teacher had moulded into a loyal and status-conscious group. It was summed up by the boy who said:

He made us feel like a sort of family.

The competition between 3A and 3B over sport, the amount of money collected for the school fund, and the number of house-points earned, combined with their form-master's efforts, created a deep solidarity in 3A which was aware of itself *as a form*. The destruction of this unity, combined with a change of form-teacher, provoked a sense of loss and wounded integrity which was resented.

Such an explanation is at best partial. More significant is the fact that the newcomers tended to deviate from or inhibit some of 4A's most basic norms. Let us consider their relative backwardness in academic achievement.

You know, those that have come up, they're not so bad, but they've slowed us down so that they can catch up. We're doing those things in Science that we were doing in second year. The lads are all right themselves, but they're a bit slow, like.

Some of them are a bit stupid. 15 and 30. I don't think they should be in [our class]. 30's smashing at general knowledge, but I don't think he and 15 should be in. They mess about.

They lag behind, like. They're slowing us down. They've not done the work the same as we have. We have to wait for them to catch up instead of getting on to new work. It means more work for us even though we've done it. We get bored in Maths. We keep going over the same work, over and over again. We keep having to wait for them to get up to standard. They never did it. And they haven't the faintest idea. We did it about a year ago and they're just starting it now. We had a test this morning that we done once in 2A.

We used to do things quicker in 3A. Now we're just going over things we've done before. They should have split the class up, you know, then we could have gone on more instead of going back with them out of other classes.

In a very real sense, yet unintentionally, the newcomers deviated from the 4A norm requiring effort towards high academic achievement. Not only had the newcomers destroyed the unity of the old 3A, but they also inhibited the progress that would otherwise have been made. These two factors, their intrusion into the form and their inhibition of academic progress, are thus inter-related and mutually reinforcing. The outcome is the tendency for the leaders to reject the newcomers as deviants.

We're not really keen on the lads who've come up. The old 3A's still there really. They think they're in the form but they're not really.

Well, Adrian and us sort of shut them out, you know what I mean?

It'll be smashing next year, 'cos there aren't many of the lads who came up staying on. You know, it's the original 3A who're staying on.

It is important to note that the newcomers' deviation from the academic norm was only partial: the newcomers were willing to work hard, but their relative backwardness retarded the form as a whole. The newcomers naturally shared the value of academic achievement, since without this they would not have shown interest in preparing for the C.S.E., but their assiduity was insufficient. This *apparent* lack of industry led some members of 4A to accuse them of using the C.S.E. as an excuse for rising into the A stream merely in the hope of obtaining a more favourable report/reference when their schooling was terminated.

These were not the only norms to which the newcomers failed to conform. In the following analysis we will be able to detect the prevailing group norm in 4A by examining the further reasons for the rejection of the newcomers: it is through their complaints of deviation that the core members of 4A make their norms or values explicit.

15 (Alf) was the most rejected member of the form: ten boys noted their dislike of him (Q.2). In other words, he was an outstanding deviant. An exception amongst the newcomers, he would not settle down to his work according to the group standard. Very quickly he acquired the reputation of a 'messer', that is someone who misbehaves when he should be working.

Alf was also a good fighter. Although he was by no means a bully, his physical exuberance and occasional aggression were not regarded favourably by the other boys. Physical aggression was not one of 4A's normatively prescribed activities. Unlike the other fourth year forms, 4A found themselves unable to name the best fighter in the form.

> I don't know who's the best fighter. In 4A, you know, they're not interested in fighting, most of them.

> If you kept fighting, they wouldn't talk to you.

Fighting *ability* in no way enhanced a boy's prestige among his peers; aggressive *activity* broke the group norm. Thus Alf was of very low informal status – rank 25.

We may regard the proscription of fighting and 'messing' as a corollary of the norm demanding great efforts towards academic achievement: to 'mess' is to inhibit everyone's progress and undermine the good teacher-pupil relationships which the form sought. Alf and Alan (16) were the leading 'messers'.

> We do get rowdy sometimes. But it's always the same people all the time . . . We tell them to shut up or else the teacher'll come in, but they just say 'Shut up' and don't pay attention to you.

> As soon as the teacher's gone out, that's when they start talking. They won't carry on with their work. I liked the proper 3A, the old 3A. It was much better. The class has got more rowdy now. Since they came up, like, they've set all the class off. Yes, Alf and them. 09, he didn't used to be like that. He tries to act real hard, like, dead tough. It's 'cos he's going with Alf and Alan. He's not tough really, he just tries to act like that.

Here we can see that 'messing' not only prevented progress in work. It also involved an implicit rejection of the status and authority of the leaders, and endangered the 'trust' relationship they had developed with teachers, who felt that they could leave the room whilst 4A boys continued with their work.

Alan was the Scottish boy who came to the school during the third year. He had great difficulty in becoming integrated into the form: his Scottish nationality and accent made him 'different'.

His lack of acceptance into 3A is coincident with his rejection of their norms.

He does his work, but he wouldn't do it if he didn't have to. He wants to leave school as soon as he possibly can. Same as some others. They're the same ones that came nowhere in class.

He was thus frequently criticized by pupils and teachers. Occasionally the teacher's awareness of, and collusion with, the boys' dislike of Alan became evident.

—'What's that huge book on your desk, Alan? Is it a dictionary?
—No, sir, it's a music book.
—What are you doing with that? Where did you get it from? Out of the library?
—Yes.
—Well just you take it straight back into there. I don't want it coming back covered with greasy chip and what have you. You can't take reference books out of the library. You must come and look at it at lunch-time. And from what I've heard you ought to be spending your time on Science, not Music. In any case, how were you going to get it home if it rained? You haven't got one of those plastic cases like the rest of the class. Where are you going to wrap it up? In a kilt or something?'

Note how the teacher ridicules Alan's Scottish origins and highlights his failure to carry books in a briefcase, which was accepted practice in 4A.

Such boys thus complained that they were 'picked on' by the teachers.

I don't like Mr. ———. He's always picking on me. 09 was once talking to the boy behind, but he brought me out and I said I wasn't doing anything but he said he saw me and so he caned me. And then he sent me out [of the room].

We were going on the bus to games. [Two of the A clique] were talking. 'Alf', [the teacher] said, 'Are you talking? Stop it.' I said I weren't and he said, 'Stop giving your cheek and shut up.' Then there was someone else talking and he picked on me and said, 'It was you that time, Alf.' He's always picking on me.

Every attempt by boys like Alan and Alf to assert themselves were firmly rebuffed.

Alf thinks he knows it all, so he just larks about and that. When we were coming here to see you, I said to ——— 'Are you coming?' and he (Alf) says, 'I'll come.' I says to him, 'You're not, you can't come', so he says, 'Well, try and stop me.' He's like that all the time. [Alf]'s a big one. He throws his weight about. He thinks everybody likes him.

A high standard of physical hygiene and dress was maintained by 4A boys. The majority dressed fairly conventionally in sports jackets or sweater, grey trousers and tie. Jeans were worn in very exceptional circumstances, and never by high status boys. Undoubtedly the leading exponent of current fashions was Adrian. Whereas most of the boys came to school in the same jacket and trousers until they had to be replaced, Adrian made frequent mid-week changes in his clothing. He followed 'Mod' fashions, with suede boots, narrow trousers, leather jackets and so on. Adrian's pride in his appearance was imitated by most of the form; indeed, it was the only form in the school where more than half the boys wore a tie. On those occasions when the form was taken out of school on a visit to some local place of interest, high standards of dress became specially important and the wearing of a suit was favoured. From these norms, Alf and Alan, amongst others, were significant deviants.

I like to keep smart at school. If you don't, they go behind your back and say 'Scruffy' or something like that. If I came without a tie or in jeans, they'd say, 'Look at him in jeans.' It's like Alf. He smells a bit with B.O. you know. He can't help it. And they, you know, sort of sniff and then pull faces behind his back.

Alf is never smart. Even when we go on a trip he doesn't go very smart. We should be smart when we go outside school.

Alf doesn't try. He's got a suit and that, but he doesn't try to alter himself. He just comes like a dustman.

Look at Alan. He was wearing a donkey-jacket when we went on that trip.

In 4A high attendance at school was normative. In part this is a reflection of the academic norm, since frequent absence is a threat to individual and group progress. But high attendance increased the form's chance of winning the Attendance Shield, which was presented to the Form Captain in Assembly with the reward of being released from school some fifteen minutes before the rest of the school. The high status boys carefully enforced this attendance norm.

Everyone in our form is anxious if someone's late. We question them when they come back and find out why they've been away.

As usual, the norm was infringed by the low status members like Alan and Alf.

Alan's the only one who's been late. And he only lives round the corner. Once he didn't come for a week and he said he had no shoes. If he'd had no shoes, he'd only stay off for a day. Then he said he was staying off to see the Olympics. 10 rushed home to see it at dinner-time, didn't you?

You know, I have to put on one of those acts when I'm told to go to school and I don't want to. Like when I stay off 'cos we're having woodwork. I say I'm going to die and all that, so I have to stay off and see the doctor.

(Alf)

In these ways, the newcomers and the low informal status ex-3A boys tended to break one or more of the form's norms. Although it is true that they were much more integrated into the form by the end of the academic year, only one boy, 04, was ever fully accepted. He and 11 (who was linked to B clique) were the only two newcomers among the twelve boys to remain at school for a fifth year. Alf and Alan left at the earliest opportunity, the end of the Easter Term 1965.

The presence of the newcomers in 4A was a situation fraught with insecurity. Witness their early comments on the tensions of the situation, their growing perception of the group norms, their desires to conform, and their need to have their conformity recognized.

Being a new class you've got to find a way of adapting to it. We're not sure how they work and how we fit in like.

We felt a bit out of it, 'cos they've done work that we've not done before.

At first a lot wouldn't bother with us. We got the usual fools who started making wise-cracks. Saying things about your face and that. But this is serious. They mean it. It's not just a joke.

It's quieter, you know. Last year all the class was getting into trouble for making a noise and things like that, and all the teachers seemed to be looking out for it.

They speak different too. Things like foul language. They don't swear much in 4A.

They dress better than us. They all wear trousers [i.e. not jeans]. We could tell that the first day we came in. They kept commenting on our clothes. And the way we had our hair and things like that.

The waistcoat I had on the other day. You know, Adrian was jealous and all that 'cos he's nearly always the best dressed lad in the class. He didn't take any notice while I had it on 'cos it was sort of very bright. He couldn't get one 'cos I got mine in Bradford, so he didn't even look at me.

This last incident illustrates the dangers of *over*conformity. The boy is acting as a threat to Adrian's position as style-setter in clothes and is snubbed because he steps out of his low status role.

The reactions of the newcomers were not all the same, as has already been indicated. Some became highly conformist to the prevailing norms, despite their general failure to acquire even moderate informal status. Others, like Alf, became deviants who rejected the high status, norm-enforcing boys, like Adrian, with the same violence with which they themselves were rejected.

Ooooo. I'll swear here. Adrian's a bum, he's a shithouse. He's like a girl. Have you seen him in the prefects' entrance. He says, 'Come on, you've got to get out.' If you hit him once he'd scream murder and run home for his Mam. He's all mouth, and that's all he is . . . I think he's one of the top boys in the class but I don't know how they can get on with him. I'd strangle him if I'd got some rope.

Thus far our discussion has been two-edged: through an

examination of the disparities between the high and low informal status members the more prominent elements of the norm content and pressures have become explicit. Conflict reveals the dominant values for in such situations the norms are expressed and re-inforced in the pressures which are brought to bear on deviants. In 4A most of the norms are expressions of the value which upholds effort towards academic achievement. Not all of these can be mentioned here, but one will be important when we consider comparative practices in other forms

In Lumley, as in most British schools, copying work from another pupil is frowned upon by teachers. The principle is that every boy must do his own work independently; failure to do this is defined as cheating. The view of teachers was fully reflected in the prevailing norm in 4A.

Copying is like cheating.

A boy was thus neither expected to copy off another boy, nor to allow another boy to copy off him. Explanation of the problem or *checking* are, however, entirely legitimate.

You can help someone to learn how to do it, but not copy the answer.

I'd tell someone how to do it, but I wouldn't show him the answer.

You can ask how to do it, but we wouldn't show you the answer. Unless you were just checking. Checking's all right.

Such was the normative structure which regulated life in 4A. The social world of 4B was very different.

FORM 4B

Our analysis must be based once again on the friendship struc-ture among the boys, which is presented in Chart II. In com-parison with 4A, the clique structure is less well defined, since only one group possesses a high proportion of reciprocated choices. Of the total number of choices made to members of the same form, 55 per cent are mutual in 4B, whereas in 4A the comparable figure is 75 per cent. In other words, the choices are spread more widely than in 4A: boys are less bound to

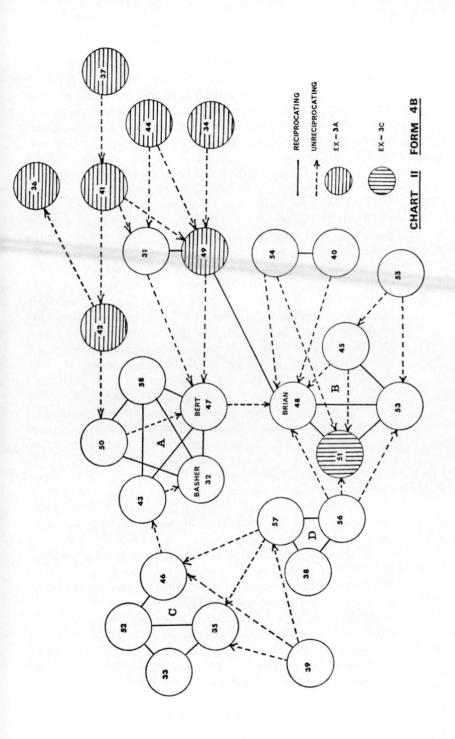

RECIPROCATING
UNRECIPROCATING

EX – 3A

EX – 3C

CHART II   FORM 4B

particular friends. The consequence is a more diffuse clique structure.

The most closely bound network of friends is Clique A, of which only one boy chooses a person external to the group. Clique A has the highest informal status rank average of 7·4, but the academic average is 15·4. None of the members was elected a prefect, and only one, 50, was a member of one of the school's First Teams. The central member of the clique is 47 (Bert), who receives six choices from other boys.

In the informal status test, three boys shared the top rank, 47 (Bert), 48 (Brian) and 32 (Basher). As the year progressed, these three boys became more closely tied by friendship than the Chart indicates, where the three are linked by Bert, and Brian does not reciprocate choices with either of the other two. Clique B consists of the four boys who centre round Brian, the most popular boy in the form in terms of number of choices received. Brian was one of the most able footballers in the school, a quality he shared with Adrian of 4A. The informal status rank average for Clique B is 11·0 and its academic average is 16·3 both scores being lower than in Clique A. Only one number, 51, who entered the form from 3C, was a prefect.

Cliques A and B are inter-locked by the developing friendship between the three highest informal status members, Brian, Bert and Basher. They also serve as a focus to many other groups and individuals. We may note, for example, the way in which 49, a boy from 3A, chooses both Brian *and* Bert.

Clique C, comprising four members, is the most likely candidate for the term 'intellectual' clique, with its academic average of 10·3, two of the ranks being under 5. Its informal status average is 14·8. The two high academic rankers were also prefects.

The three boys in Clique D obtained moderate informal status and academic averages of 15·7 and 18·7 respectively. This was a quiet, unassuming group of boys, who like the members of Clique C were favoured by the teachers.

4B, like 4A, received a large number of newcomers at the beginning of the year. Seven boys came from 3A and one from 3C. Whereas the 3C boy is fully integrated into the high status B clique, only one of the ex-3A boys has been well integrated into the form by the end of the Autumn term when these sociometric data were collected. They tend to choose one another, rather than ex-3B boys; only one boy receives a choice from a former 3B boy; three are isolates, remaining unchosen even by other ex-3A boys. It is interesting that three of these boys choose 49, who is the only ex-3A boy to be chosen by an ex-3B boy: he does in fact receive a reciprocated choice from Brian. It is as if the newcomers are tending to cluster round the one member who has become accepted into the form. Of the original 3B members, two, 55 and 39, are isolates; as we shall see their rejection was indicative of their non-conformity to the group's norms.

Of course, the structure changed slightly over time. The three high status boys became closer friends; the ex-3A boys became more integrated, especially with the high-status boys; the deviants too began to cluster, especially in the later friendship between the isolate 39 and 33 of Clique C. Most relevant to our discussion is the fact that the newcomers did not become the rejected deviants of 4B. There are two main reasons for this. Firstly, the newcomers to 4B were like the core-members in their lack of interest in the C.S.E. They had been demoted to 3B because of their intention not to take the C.S.E. and the low academic positions they had occupied in 3A. In other words, the values of the ex-3A group were consonant with those of the ex-3B boys in that their intentions were not strikingly academic; they were all 'leavers' who would end their schooling as soon as they reached the statutory age. Secondly, investigation showed that these ex-3A boys were highly conformist to the norms imposed by the high status 3B boys. To what extent their conformity is the result of rapid adaptation to a new form, or of attitudes they already held whilst in the lowest academic positions in 3A is difficult to determine; no doubt their conformity is a function of both.

The somewhat 'non-academic' attitudes of the ex-3A boys are clear from the following comments.

I liked it 3A. But we didn't mess about, did we? They were all right. Some used to mess about – like Adrian and Arnold – but *we* used to get caned. They got away with it.

Adrian and Arnold used to mess, but they got away with it, like. [The teacher] used to sort of pick on us. If owt was missing, they'd go to us straightaway, wouldn't they?

We were the dead ends of the class. We never came anywhere in the class.

Adrian and Arnold and 37 were teacher's pets in 3A. And 23 [A clique member in 4A]. They used to get round [the form teacher]. They used to ask him did he want owt doing. So if they did owt [wrong] they didn't get done.

They [4A] are always criticizing, you know, everyone that's come down [into 4B]. 49, you know, his hair and all that. You know, moaning at him. Calling him a dead lot.

The central concern here is the value of 'messing' combined with their rejection of Adrian and Arnold as 'pets'. It seems that in 3A and 4B these boys perceived 'messing' as an attractive activity. In the A stream such behaviour was highly deviant, leading to low informal status: in 4B, as we shall see, such behaviour was conformist, leading to high informal status. The newcomers tended, therefore to view their new form with considerable favour; there are few signs of conflict or insecurity.

It's more fun in this class – with Bert. It's a lot different from 3A. It wouldn't be the same without Bert.

We have a lot of fun. *They know when to have some fun in this class, and when not to.* When the teacher's not there. But with some you can mess about even when they're in.

We're not picked on in 4B. Mr. —— chucked me out though. Twice, the same period each week. I'd just finished the poem or summat and got up to tell him that I'd finished and he just started bawling and sent me out, didn't he?

4B's better than the A class. It's more fun. The A class just sit there. They're soft. You can't have a giggle with them. With taking the exam they have to be quiet and all that. In our class you can have a giggle.

That this 'having fun' value represents conformity to the central norm of 4B, either in the form of an adaptation and/or an agreement between the inherent attitudes of the newcomers and the 'culture' of 4B, will be clear from the comments of ex-3B boys.

We don't like boys who don't mess about.

We don't like boys who answer a lot of questions. If you answer all the questions, the lesson goes all the quicker, doesn't it? I mean, say you have two periods and you start having all these questions, right, then it would take a period to do, and then you have another period and then you'd have to do some new work. If they start asking questions and we don't answer them they have to start explaining it all to us and it takes two periods. So we don't have to use the pen.

If the teachers ask *you*, you usually tell them the answer. If they don't ask *you*, you just keep quiet.

I've liked the fun in this class best. It's Bert mostly. He's dead comical. He's always getting done. Well, he don't bother about getting done. He's always pulling faces and making up names and all that.

It's more noisy in 4B so it's more fun. They get caned in our class more than they do in 4A. It's Bert who gets caned most.

And then somebody sat down and couldn't get up 'cos there was glue on the seat. They plastered it on their hands and then they'd say, Hi, and shake hands with you. It was [so] doing that. And Basher. He was sticking pencils in the glue.

The values held by the high status members of 4B thus form a marked contrast with those exhibited by high status 4A boys. The pressure towards high academic achievement yields to a philosophy of 'having fun', and this was particularly exemplified by Bert.

You'd think Bert would have learn his lesson by now. You know, he shouts everything, calls, throws pencils, pens and rulers about, but if he gets caught he seems to be the only one who gets caught. Like when he stole those books. There was a lot more than him stole them. There's about eight at least. But he's the only one that gets caught.

He gets the cane. But as soon as he comes back he starts talking again. He doesn't seem to learn anything from getting belted. It doesn't do him any good getting hit in this way. He takes hundreds of beltings. He's so used to it he doesn't care if he gets caned.

Bert accepted his punishments happily, since this was the price he paid for his high status, which was derived mainly from the fact that his clowning allowed others to 'have fun' without incurring direct penalties. The teachers' punishments were ineffective since to abandon this *modus vivendi* would cause Bert to lose his prestige.

The 'non-academic' norm is reflected in other ways, for example in copying.

A lot of boys copy in the exams. It helps you if you copy, doesn't it? I mean if you see the teachers answer paper you don't just wrap it up and throw it in the dust-bin, do you?

We all copy as much as we can. If a lad doesn't let you copy we call him tight.

If I can do it, I do it on my own, but if I can't I copy.

Most people will let you copy. We don't mind really, 'cos we copy off them.

31 comes round to my house of a Sunday and gets the book off me so he can copy it. He says, 'I'll take it to our house then you won't forget to bring it to school tomorrow.'

You can do more messing here and I've come higher in the class you know. And they'll let you copy and things like that, but there was only a couple who'd let you copy in 3A.

Bert never listens but he copies off 58. He might know one of the ten [sums] but he'll copy off 58 and he might get eight or nine [right]. But he don't know owt about it. Then when the teacher asks him he looks round the class for someone to tell him. I think the teacher knows but he never says owt about it.

43 copies off me [52]. He says, 'Oh come one, I told you an answer in woodwork. Come on, you've got to tell me an answer in English.' He copies them all off and then says, when he gets into maths, 'Come on, I told you some more answers in woodwork so tell me some more answers in Maths.' You know things like that.

Most times 4A's books are in the desks underneath, so you can pull them out and copy the answers.

When I asked one boy what would happen if a boy refused to allow someone to copy I was told:

> Well, the lad he'd turned down would think, 'He's no good him, I don't like him' – you know – and about a week later the same thing would happen again and then he'd call him tight or something like that. And it would go round the class that he's a tight lad, you see. Then he'd be ignored, you see. After about three weeks the lad's getting fed up of this, so he lets them copy and he comes back into the family as you might say.

The sanctions and pressures against refusing to allow another boy to copy are clearly indicated in these extracts. Deviants are labelled as 'tight' or simply ignored. Such potential threats represent powerful pressures towards conformity to the group norms from which boys basically derive their status, and rejection of those teacher values which confer relatively much less status.

In 4A, explaining the problem or 'checking' the results was entirely normative in the peer group. In contrast, copying directly is quite legitimate in 4B and is not regarded as a form of cheating. Indeed arrangements for mutual exchange are organized, leading to permanent relationships of obligation. Deviants are rejected and consequently lose informal status. It is true that some of the more academically orientated boys were *secretly* opposed to copying, and inconsistent in the favours they granted in this respect, but they rarely resisted completely. For this reason, 46, one of the most academic boys in the form, was able to achieve informal status rank 6, as his comments show.

> It's mostly copying in homework. And in exams I don't think they're strict enough. Like, Bert. Say out of 200 [marks] he might get 150 in the exams, but if it had been like a mock exam in the hall and [the arrangement of desks] had been spread out more, he might only have got 50. It looks so obvious. Like in English. Mr. ———'s always moaning about not copying in tests. He's always saying things like this; he's walking round the room and Bert's sat there like this, looking at the other person's paper, writing it all down, or looking behind him and getting the answers and Mr. ——— just walks right past him. He never seems to do anything about it.

I don't mind people copying, but I think they're daft doing it. If we did have a real test, you know, with a lot of watching so you don't copy, well he won't have much of a chance 'cos he'll know nothing. He'll get a low mark and that's it. *But you don't like to say no if he wants to copy.*

The norm in 4B is most adequately regarded as '*non*-academic' rather than '*anti*-academic', for the boys did not completely reject the value of academic achievement. The majority of the boys who were staying at Lumley until the end of the Summer Term were glad that they were taking the Local Leaving Certificate at the end of the year, since they believed that this would help them to obtain a better job than would be possible for those 4C and 4D boys who could not take the examination. Academic work was never regarded as valuable for its own sake: it was purely a means to a better job. [6] The norm permitted considerable deviance from the teachers' expectations of what a 4B boy should achieve or how he should behave, but it did prescribe a *minimum* of academic effort. 'Playing the fool' is seen more as a *relief* from hard work, not a *replacement* of it.

It's better not working hard then you can have some fun.

But the whole concept of working hard was not abandoned· Whereas the 4A boys had to work harder than was necessary for the Leaving Certificate Examination because of their intention to take the C.S.E., 4B boys had the one examination and earlier leaving as their goal. 'Having fun' is the difference permitted by the unequal standards expected by the teachers from the two forms, and from the A-B distinction.

If you're in 4A, the teachers expect you to set a standard, you know? But if you're in 4B the teachers almost expect you to be that bit more stupid, you know what I mean?

In 4A attendance figures were high. The increased absence rate for 4B undoubtedly represents the lack of pressure exerted by the non-academic norms. One ex-3A boy explained the difference.

It was different in 3A. They'd say, 'Yeah, spoilt our attendance! We won't get out at a quarter to four now.' But it's not like that in 4B.

Fighting ability was irrelevant to informal status in 4A, and its display led to loss of prestige. In 4B Basher was indisputably the best fighter and Brian the second best. Fights were very rare in this form. One boy did challenge Brian, but the fight was stopped by a teacher. Since the challenge was never repeated, Brian's position as second best fighter remained secure. High status in 4B is thus associated with 'messing' and fighting ability. The three boys at the top of the informal status hierarchy exhibited these, but Bert specialized in the former, and Basher and Brian in the latter. But there was little bullying or 'pushing around' in 4B with the exception of the deviants. 'Having fun' required friendly relationships among the boys and such a situation was inconsistent with bullying. Rather, the importance of fighting ability was recognized, but its display was not permitted. As one boy with average informal status expressed it:

They mess around but they don't act big. They're funny. You can have a laugh when you're with them.

The high status fighters demanded that their fighting ability should be acknowledged, but they avoid the danger of becoming 'bigheaded' through its gratuitous display.

The leaders of 4A were notably smart in appearance. Different norms were current in 4B.

Them in 4A call you and that. They say things about you. You know, your clothes and things like that. Adrian and Arnold. They're always criticizing. Arnold'll say, 'Oh look your shoes are dirty.' But in this class they don't bother, 'cos nearly everybody's got dirty shoes. Most of the class have.

I'd put a tie on to this exhibition thing on Monday but not if I was just walking about the street.

Wearing a tie's thick. School ones are old-fashioned – they're wide and come to a point.

They call you if you've got a tie on.

I like my collar open all the time. And I wear one of those tee-shirts. And ties chokes you, so I don't like them.

Uniforms are thick. I didn't want a uniform when I came here.

They look funny. If we had one I wouldn't wear it out of school.

Long hair's great. It suits some people. Like 49.

We'd nearly all have our hair long if all the teachers didn't go on about it.

These bags are all right to keep your stuff in when it's raining. But they're not worth it, are they?

It is as if ties, uniforms, brief-cases and short hair styles are the symbols of A stream academicism, with which these B boys did not wish to be associated. The high status boys tended to have long hair, especially Basher, and to come to school in jeans from time to time. Both practices were opposed by the teachers. Yet some high status academically orientated boys such as 46 were 'permitted' to have short hair and ties, since they conformed to the more basic norms.

The norms we have considered emerge again in reference to the deviants:

We wouldn't throw a rubber at 37. He's too quiet, you know. Some people are touchy as well.

55 tells on you. He told on me this morning. They're no good, are they, if they tell on you?

We don't like boys who work hard. That's soft. We'd tell him we didn't like him. Smash! We'd mess about with him and shake him like we do with 55.

55 with girls! He says 'disgraceful' and all that. Dead long words about it.

33 and 39 wear ties. We call 33 and 39. But not 52. He's all right him.

57 in our class wears a tie. He thinks he's brainy. You've got a tie and you're brainy, aren't you?

They're all smart in 4A, but there's only a couple who're smart in our class. You know, 33 and 39.

36 might not lend me his [book]. He'd let you copy but he wouldn't let you take his book back to your seat. 33 and 39

wouldn't let you copy. But all the rest would. Oh, 40 wouldn't 'cos everybody's always hitting him.

I wouldn't lend mine to 33 or 39. I don't like them. They think they're great at everything.

In these statements the relation between non-conformity to the dominant norms and rejection is exposed. The extent of the rejection of deviants can be verified by a review of their place in the friendship structure of the form. 55 and 37 are complete isolates. Isolate 39 and 33 formed a strong friendship tie during the Spring Term. 55 was rejected by no less than fourteen boys on the dislike question. The average informal status rank of the boys mentioned above is 24·5 : not one of them has a rank higher than 20. In interview, their non-conformity was openly confessed.

We've got some bigheads and they sort of upset things. They're always mucking about. Showing off.

The noisy ones are mostly Bert, 50, Basher and Brian, you know people like that. If it weren't for them it would be a quiet class. It annoys us. When you're trying to do something it gets on your wick. You can only tell them to shut up and sometimes that only makes it worse.

We don't copy. When we've done I ask 33 what he's got and then we see if we've got the same answers. But we don't copy. And if we don't get the same answer we run through it and see where we've gone wrong, I mean it might be me or it might be 33.

(39)

I don't like that sort of thing. My dad's always going on about that. He says, 'If you get them wrong, don't copy them.'

There are some in our class that ought to be in 4C. You know, them as don't work.

It used to be fairly good in our class until the others come down. Bert didn't used to be too bad, but when that lot come down, it all went worse, and Bert was always getting done and getting the class a bad name.

Boys in 4B, who took the Local Leaving Certificate in the fourth year, are intermediate between 4A boys, who took the

Local Leaving Certificate and in some cases the C.S.E. in the fifth year, and boys in 4C and 4D, who took no examinations at all. Likewise, the normative structure of 4B is a compromise between the academic values of 4A and the anti-academic norms we shall observe in 4C and 4D. We may term these 4B norms non-academic since although 'messing' is an approved activity, there is no attempt to replace academic work with misbehaviour, nor are academically orientated boys necessarily subjected to low status.

FORM 4C

In this form, as indicated in Chart III, the friendship structure divides naturally into three distinct cliques, between which there are no inter-linking choices. In this respect 4C differs from the two forms described so far, where each group tends to be connected to the others. 69 per cent of the in-form choices are reciprocated.

Clique A is rather loosely organized if assessed by the relatively low proportion of reciprocated choices. In this respect Chart III is misleading, for this clique is one half of the real group formed by a combination of the A cliques from 4C and 4D, (see Chart V). This combination will be considered as a whole at a later stage; for the moment, we are concerned with the form as a separate entity. Clique A consists of a pair, 74 and 67, and a larger group of five boys which is connected to the pair by 84's unreciprocated choice of 74, and one 'aspirant' boy, 68. The average informal status rank of the group is very high, 5·9: the clique in fact contains the top six ranks, the first three being occupied by 74 (Clint), 84 (Clem) and 67 respectively. The academic average for the group is 13·5. No member was a prefect or a First Team player.

Clique B is characterized by its high proportion of reciprocated choices. It consists of five members and one 'aspirant', 81. Of the three boys who came from 3B, only 71 has become fully integrated into the group. The informal status rank average is 9·8, and the academic average, 15·3, is slightly lower than that of the A clique. None of these boys was a prefect, but 61 was one of the most able football players in the school.

Clique C really comprises three subgroups: a quartet, a triad

34

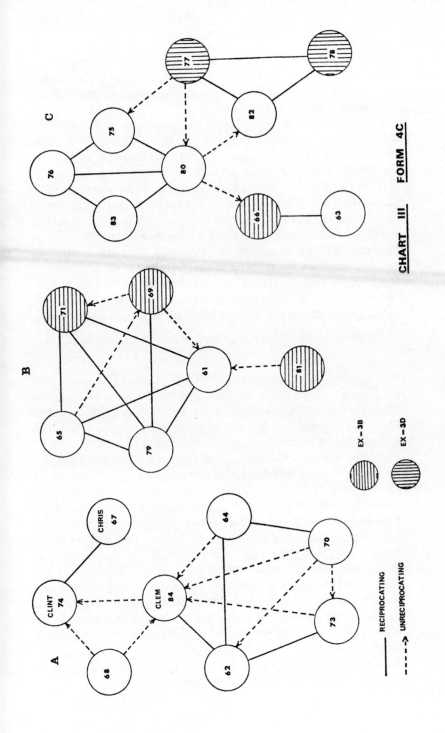

RECIPROCATING
------> UNRECIPROCATING

A

CHRIS 67

CLINT 74

68

CLEM 84

64

70

73

62

B

71

69

65

61

79

81

EX – 3B

EX – 3D

C

77

78

75

82

76

80

83

66

63

CHART III   FORM 4C

and a pair, which are inter-linked by unreciprocated choices. Its informal status rank average is the lowest of the three cliques, 18·5, but its academic rank average, 8·4, is by far the highest. Two boys, 75 and 63, were prefects.

In a word, the first two cliques have high informal status, but a low academic average; the C clique has a low informal status but a high academic average. We shall see how these facts are indicators of the normative process within the form.

That the key figure in 4C is Clint (74) is not obvious from Chart III. He makes only one in-form choice and is chosen by three others. However, he occupies the top rank on informal status. The history of Clint's rise to the pinnacle of the prestige hierarchy will be described in detail at a later stage; for our present purposes we must note that by the fourth year he was 'cock of the school', that is, he was accepted as the best fighter. No other boy at Lumley was prepared to challenge him to a fight.

Clint summarized the A clique's attitude to school when he said:

> I think school's a waste of time. If I don't like a lesson, I don't do it.

The behavioural counterpart of this attitude was fully confirmed by my own observation of this clique in lessons. During one Mathematics lesson, all the 4C boys were working from various sections of the text-book. Clint as usual was sitting next to Chris, surrounded by other A clique members. Throughout the lesson Clint never opened his book or used his pen. The time was spent in gossiping, day-dreaming, combing his hair and threatening smaller boys in the form. During Library periods, he wasted the majority of his time in an apparent search for a book, playing hide-and-seek with the teacher behind the partitions. For Clint, any form of academic work was irksome; it would be avoided scrupulously and flagrantly. Yet Clint was, by the eleven plus results, one of the more intelligent boys in the school. His ingenuity for avoiding getting into trouble with the teachers was remarkable. More often he would goad other boys into pranks which inevitably led to a rebuke or punishment from the teacher. When a situation seemed unlikely to provoke retaliation from the teacher, Clint lost no opportunity to break the rules. This approach produced a norm which forbade any kind of academic achievement to his followers.

You throw things at your mates, 'cos they take it as a joke and throw things back.

I like 79 'cos he's always messing about. We get a lot of laughs out of him.

The nature of 'messing' as defined by 4C members forms a close parallel to that in 4B, but there are important differences. The practice of copying is a good example.

We don't like people who won't let you copy.

65's the only one who does any work really [in the B clique]. So we all copy his book. You know, if we've been mucking about.

It's tight if he wouldn't let you copy. No one would take any notice of him. They wouldn't talk to him.

Thus far the situation is similar to that in 4B. The difference is that in 4B 'messing' is seen as an enjoyable activity, which relieves the lesson of its monotony. Copying becomes a necessity, since it satisfies the teacher and allows the boys to obtain marks and maintain their academic position. Moreover, in 4B copying is practised by means of mutual obligations. Arrangements for the mutual exchange of information are organized. Not so in 4C. There is no wish for any academic achievement by copying: its purpose is purely to deceive the teacher into the belief that the work is being done. Secondly, most of the copying is not based on mutual exchange between friends. Rather, members of clique A would *force* by threat or actual aggression members of clique C to divulge the answers or loan the book. As one A clique boy put it:

It's no use copying off 64 'cos when he does the sums he gets them wrong. I copy off [three C clique members].

I copy off 75 [in the C clique]. He's supposed to be the brainiest in the class. He couldn't stop me 'cos I'd smash him and take the book.

They just take the book. He wouldn't ask you for it. He'd say, 'Give it me or I'll hit you.'

(C clique member).

This fact was amply supported by my own observations. On one occasion when I was present during a mathematics lesson of 4C, Clint spent most of the lesson walking around the room, throwing rulers, stealing everyone's blotting paper and punching the smaller boys. After a time he sat down next to 79. The class was being taught how to do logarithms. Clint began to copy from 65, the most hard-working member of Clique B. Several tussles ensued as Clint snatched the book and copied the sums into his own. When the teacher wrote up the answers on the board, Clint said:

Are them the answers?

and proceeded to copy the one he had not completed into his book. Simultaneously, 64 and 62 of the A clique were copying from the book belonging to 76 of Clique C. At one stage Clint turned round to 65 and said 'Come on, do number two for us'. The lesson proceeded for some time in this fashion. Eventually the teacher began to mark the boy's work. When 65's book was examined the teacher was very angry since the boy had been using the antilogarithms for the logarithms. He found the same error, naturally, when he marked the work of Clint and 79, who had copied from Clint, but the teacher ignored, or was unaware of, the cause of this.

Although forcibly taking a book from one of the C Clique was prevalent among A Clique boys other methods of copying were discovered. A favourite method in subjects like Maths was to write the date in the exercise book in pencil so that on a future occasion this could be erased with a rubber and the current date substituted, so that work completed or copied previously would appear contemporaneous.

The rejection of the academic approach was thus much more marked in 4C than in 4B. Whereas in 4B the group solution was to compromise between working hard and completely wasting time, in 4C the solution was a total abandonment of academic values. In this sense the 4C norm was *anti*-academic. This is clearly expressed by the low status deviants of the C clique who did work hard:

Myself, I think if they come top in something, I think they think the others will go away from them. You know, 'He's getting soft' and all that.

They don't work very hard in our class. When we're doing

Maths., they just copy and then talk for the rest of the time. They think it's all the same if you copy.

They can't stand seeing anyone get on with their work.

In this class they're always acting daft, just so as they can keep in with their mates.

I'm sure if one of them put his head in the fire and they thought it was good, they'd all do the same.

There are too many messers. They won't let you get on with your work.

The others are too fond of messing about and doing no work. Not bothering about learning anything. I like doing work 'cos when I leave school I want to go to night-school to be an electrician.

In 4B the norm was against working *too* hard, that is, failing to make full use of opportunities for 'messing' which bring relief from work. In 4C, the norm is against working *at all*: 'messing' is the alternative to work. The only exception to the norm is during the end of term examinations, when an effort is made lest the boy should be demoted to 4D.

The norms concerning dress are similar to those of 4B in that ties are forbidden, i.e. laughed at; they are extended in that the wearing of jeans is encouraged.

I wouldn't wear a tie if they tried to make me. I don't have one.

They'd take the mickey out of a lad that came in a tie. They wouldn't stop talking to him. They'd just take the mickey out of him for a bit.

Lots of boys in our class come to school in jeans but you hardly ever see 4A or 4B in jeans.

[The teachers] get everybody in the morning – don't they? – when we're coming into the Hall. Mr. ——— and Mr. ——— are at the door and when they see you're wearing jeans they drag you out and give you a lecture.

Signs that a boy was highly acceptable to the teachers were signs of unacceptability to the A clique.

96 is always trying to get into our group. We won't have him though. He's a prefect. He's always hanging around, you know, and we're always telling him to shut up.

I don't like my friends to be snobby or owt.

Absenteeism and truancy provoked no hostility in the high status boys. It was taken as a matter of course.

The boys don't bother here. They wouldn't say owt. They'd come for us of a night, you know, the lads I go with, and I'd still go out with them and tell them what I'd been doing all day and all that, so they hardly notice when I went back to school.

[The Headmaster] knows I have days off. He just says, 'You're another dodger, get out.'

Every time you're off, when you come they all say, 'You've been wagging it: you've not been ill.' They know, but they'd never tell the teachers.

The members of the C clique, of course, failed to conform to the norms set by the high status boys. They worked hard; they behaved well in class; their relations with the teachers were friendly; they dressed well; they attended school regularly. These are the roots of their low informal status in 4C.

We may consider the dominant norms in 4C as an extension of those current in 4B. The taboo against ties leads to encouragement of long hair and the wearing of jeans, both of which were against the school rules. 'Messing' becomes a substitute for work. Truancy is inconsequential. The need to copy now justifies the use of threat or force. Smoking in the school yard is a sign of status. This was the pattern of behaviour imposed by Clint, who, though by no means popular, maintained his status by his fighting ability. And since, unlike the situation in 4B, working hard would not even lead to a chance of success in the Local Leaving Certificate at the end of the year, the anti-academic forces increased in strength.

FORM 4D

In this form, the friendship structure, which is plotted in Chart IV,

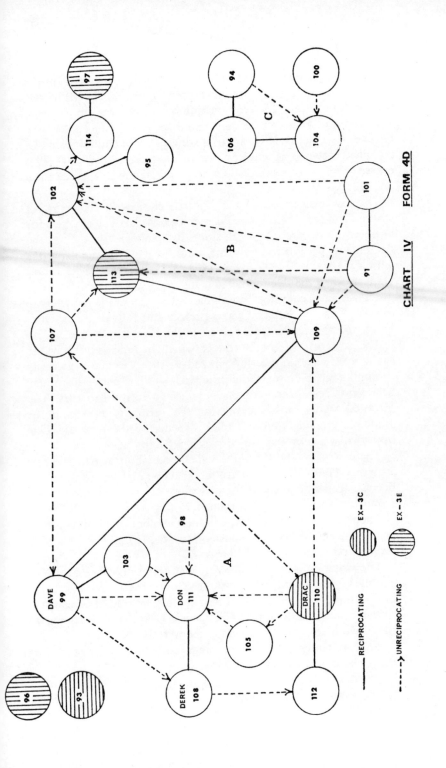

CHART IV   FORM 4D

RECIPROCATING

- - - → UNRECIPROCATING

EX—3C

EX—3E

is less clearly differentiated into cliques than in the case of 4C. The proportion of reciprocated choices, 49 per cent is the lowest for the four forms. In terms of number of choices, three boys, 111, 109 and 102, can be considered 'popular', since each boy receives six choices. If we are to distinguish two cliques from this complex network of choices, we must divide those boys who centre around 111 from those who take 109 and 102 as the focal points.

The low proportion of reciprocated choices in Clique A, of whom Don (111) is the central member, is partly accounted for by the high degree of reciprocation between this group and the A clique in 4C. For the moment, we must consider the networks within the form. Seven boys and one 'aspirant' (98) cluster round Don, to form the A clique. Their informal status average is 4·5: in fact, they occupy the top eight ranks. The academic average is 15·3. None of the boys was a prefect, but four of them, Don, Dave, 105 and Derek were players in the First Rugby Team.

The structure of the B clique, which includes nine boys, is again somewhat diffuse. It is linked to the A clique principally through 109's reciprocated choice with 99. The clique itself may be regarded as a series of inter-connected reciprocal pairs. The informal status rank average for the group is 14·8, and the academic average, 10·6, is higher than that of the A clique. One boy, 101, was a prefect, and 107 was a Rugby player.

There remains the C clique, which consists of a trio and one aspirant. Their informal status rank average is very low, 22·0, but the academic average, 12·3, is close to the B clique's score. None was a prefect or a sportsman.

The two complete isolates, who neither choose nor are chosen are significantly two of the newcomers. 96, from 4E, was both a prefect and a leading footballer.

The structure is already showing a close resemblance to that in 4C: the higher the informal status, the lower the academic average of the clique, and vice-versa. From a consideration of the normative structure of the form, it will become clear that we may regard these two forms as equivalents in many respects.

The A clique actively supports the anti-academic values described in our earlier discussion.

Our class is better than 4C. You get a better laugh. We throw rubbers at Mr. ———. Dave (99) used to hit him. But now he just doesn't give the rubbers out. We chuck clips now.

Derek's (108) taking the mickey out of Mr. ——— all the time. He stands for it an' all. He's a right scream, Derek.

If he's in a good mood Mr. ——— starts taking the mickey out of me so I start taking it out of him. I was doing my work and he thought I was mucking about so he says, 'He's writing a love-letter' and all that lot, so I started shouting out like 'Blankeye' and '[the teacher's first name]' and he got mad.

I never do much work. I just play about.

In Maths he says 'Get on with your work', but I don't.

You have more fun in fourth year. In first year you daren't say owt. But it's great fun in fourth year. You can give a dead lot of cheek, you know, 'cos you're leaving.

I wouldn't do exams. I'd rip the paper up. I wouldn't do exams and then let them say you've not passed. 'Cos I know I wouldn't pass. I'm not good enough. I'm not clever enough. It's a waste of time.

I've learnt nowt in this class.

They don't realize that while they're messing about all the time the teacher's keeping a check on them. And when it comes to the end of the year it goes on their report. I got a good report last year but they didn't. 'Messing about' and all that, that's what the teachers put on it. I'm crafty. I don't let Mr. ——— see me when I mess about.

You come to school and you do exactly nothing. You don't do much. It's not like at work where you have to do long hours. It's dead cushy this school. You don't do nowt. You're supposed to do writing but they don't check the books, so you don't have to do it.

It's 'cos you're leaving. I've just lost interest in everything. I've just stopped working and become lazy and that. I just can't wait for four o'clock and that.

I smoke nearly every day, me, Dave, Clint, 103, 62. No one's caught very often. It's just the odd one.

Once this basic attitude is defined, it hardly seems surprising that copying is rife or that force is used in the acquisition of material.

In Science I had the paper under the desk and he must have knew I had it 'cos he called me out and took it off me and made met sit out at the front.

96 and 103 had all books under the desk in that English test. I always get my book and copy a few sums off somebody else and then leave it and muck about. I copy off one at the top.

Mr. —— knows but he doesn't say owt. But he'd cane me if he saw me doing it when he's walking round. But if he just sees you from his desk he doesn't bother and lets you carry on.

He goes mad if you copy in tests. You've got to be careful then. I pass a piece of paper to someone a bit farther away and say 'Write all the answers down.'

I work one lesson, and you know, try to do as much as I can. Then I don't do nowt and I just keep putting the dates about every three sums. And you get away with it.

I'm waiting for 96 now. I've had to wait about two weeks for him to finish his corrections. I just keep going over the work I've done. You know, writing over it.

The other day he came up and looked at my book and I'd only got the date in. I didn't know what to do. He told me to do summat. So Don got hold of my book and wrote in it. About ten lines for me. And then [the teacher] came back and says, 'Oh, that's good.'

He knows 'cos when he marks it he says, 'Oh, you got someone good to copy off this time.'

Absenteeism was higher than in any of the fourth year forms except 4E. The absence rate was not, of course, spread evenly over the form[7]: 110 and 112 were absent more frequently than any of the others. But as the illustrations show, truancy was not discouraged by the other boys.

I wasn't ill when I was off. I only came back today. The woman from the Welfare shoved a note through the door like she always does, and I've put on why I was off or summat like that. So I took it to [the Headmaster] and he just told me to get out. He always does. I don't know what my Mam wrote. My Mam sent in the Medical Certificate before. I went to the doctor and told him I was having pains so he gave me a note. It's easy to get one but it costs two bob. I said I'd be in on Monday on the sick note. And I went to have some teeth out, you know, but I didn't go so I said I'd got cold in my gums. [The Headmaster] doesn't believe it all but he can't do owt.

I just stayed in the house while I was off. It's not really worth staying off. It's boring. That's when I come back, when I'm bored. It's all right staying off for a week. But if you stay off six weeks like 92, it's boring. He lives in the next street to us. He's not ill 'cos he's walking around. He's been in hospital and he keeps saying he's coming but he never does 'cos he's got a good excuse.

If I'd known that Exhibition was on I wouldn't have come back. I'd have gone there.

I never went out [of the house] for a week but in the last four days I went playing billiards in a cafe with 110. But I didn't see him all the first week. He was in his pigeon-cote. You know, in the back yard . . . I just stayed in. I just sat there reading comics. But then the School Board caught me on Friday night. She caught me on the Friday night but I said nowt so she said, 'When are you going back to school?' So I had to say Monday. But I never came on Monday. I made up an excuse that I went for a pair of shoes. I came in on Wednesday. My Mam told me not to stay off. She said she won't keep me off any more. She told me to try to keep in [school].

The return to school is effected by lack of an adequate excuse, the end to parental collusion, or boredom.

Form of dress is of little importance to the high status boys, except that wearing a tie is forbidden, and the wearing of jeans and long hair confer prestige.

The low status deviants were, of course, critical of the high status boys and their values.

That lot just mess all the time. They never do no work.

They wear tight jeans and long hair. They're scruffy, jeans. I don't like them.

The least thing you say to Dave, he hits you in the face.

They hit you but you can't hit them back, or they'll beat you up. If I hit 113 or 114 someone else'll come and beat me up.

It's no use taking our lot out on a school trip. I don't think they should. They'd be messing about and all that. Imagine taking them to a cigarette factory!

On occasions a low status boy would try to retaliate against the bullying to which he was subjected. When 100 fought back against 114, a very small boy who used the A clique's protection to support his attacks on low status boys, the result was disastrous for 100. As Derek reported:

Two of us got him in the end. He walked into the pill-hall and we grabbed him and pulled him into the toilet. This lad nutted him and his nose started bleeding, and I smashed his glasses.

The boys in 4D like those in 4C were fully aware of the differences between the cliques, and the criteria of membership. This may be illustrated by the replies to my questions about what sort of person a new boy would have to be like to be allowed to join the clique.

It depends. If he's been in trouble with the police, and he gives cheek to the teachers, he's in our group. But if he's quiet, he's not.

He'd always be messing about, not doing his work, acting hard on kids, you know what I mean?

(A clique members)

He'd have to be a good fighter, not very fond of work, go round looking for trouble and things like that. But if he didn't do that, they wouldn't let him in their group and he'd come in ours.

(B clique member)

He'd have to get on with his work, quiet, you know. And he wouldn't be acting hard in class.

46

If you don't like Dave and that lot you can go with [102 – B clique] and if they won't have you, you can go with us.

(C clique members)

These boys not only perceive the membership criteria for each clique, but they accept the prestige hierarchy involved: the low status clique must accept the rejects from those cliques with higher informal status. During the year 4D did in fact receive a new boy. Almost immediately he became an aspirant member of the A clique. He tried to impress them with stories of his delinquent acts, but he was not believed. His persistent bad behaviour in the class failed to impress. Eventually, he picked a quarrel with an A clique boy. The group provoked a fight between the new boy and one of the poorest A clique members. The new boy lost. After some time, the A clique did begin to show signs of allowing him into the group, but before this could be effected fully, the boy was sent to an approved school for theft. His first evidence of a real claim to group membership came too late.

Chapter Three

MEASUREMENT OF DIFFERENCES

One of the major problems of the social scientist is that of ascertaining that his perception and analysis of a social system does bear a close relation to what is actually occurring. The picture which has been presented so far may indeed by an accurate reflection of social processes in Lumley School, but observation and interview do not in themselves adequately safeguard our need to support what is claimed, since it is possible that what is conveyed to the reader is based on a biased selection of observations and extracts from interviews. For this reason we must try to find more 'objective' methods of reporting the situation: their function will be to act as a *measure* of the attitudes and processes we have detected and these measures can be subjected to statistical analysis.* In so doing we may be able to summarize and elaborate the normative differentiation embodied in the streaming system at Lumley School and thus furnish independent support for observation and interview material.

Perhaps the most obvious set of differences between the four fourth year forms consists of a number of dimensions which for convenience we may subsume under the heading of *differential commitment to school*. This area would include, for example, willingness to come to school, attitudes to work, to teachers, behaviour in school, and participation in school activities. Some of these dimensions, such as the teacher-pupil relationships, will

---

* A statistical test acts as a check on the *significance* of results, that is, the extent to which the results may have occurred by chance or accident. Scientists do not usually accept results as significant unless the probability of getting the results by accident is less than one in twenty (expressed as $p < 0.05$), and more often, less than one in a hundred (expressed as $p < 0.01$). Whenever we show that this probability value is low, we have good grounds for claiming that our observations do represent real trends or differences.

be treated more fully at a later stage; for the present, let us try to confirm the claims we have already made.

In our situation at Lumley School, a number of simple indicators of this differential commitment is available. Let us take one example. We have seen that the attitudes of boys to regular attendance at school vary with level of stream. For the A stream boys, there are strong pressures from the staff towards academic achievement, and thus towards regular attendance, since this supports individual and group progress; and both these values are reflected in the norms imposed by the boys themselves. In the lower streams the boys are less concerned about academic achievement or regular attendance. For the low stream boys all examinations are internal to the schools; there are thus no checks of the level of attainment reached by any external standard. There will always be one boy at the top and one at the bottom of the form in every examination, whatever the general level of attainment. The staff and boys are thus less concerned about regular attendance, since the absence of a few boys does not retard the progress of the form so obviously, nor is the teacher driving the boys towards an examination which will also assess *his* competence as a teacher by the number of 'passes' he obtains. The interconnection between teacher and pupil norms is a complex one; we cannot easily assess their relative contributions. But we can show that these forces do produce real differences in the absence rates in different streams.

The relevant figures for each of the four fourth forms are given in Table II. In each term there is a sharp increase in the absence rates as we move from the A to the D stream.[1] (The absence rates are higher for all forms in the Spring Term when there is a greater degree of illness.) We may conclude that the higher the stream, the lower the absence rate, a finding which confirms our analysis of the norms in each form. (A fuller account of the absence rates is given in Appendix II.)

There is, of course, an alternative explanation of these figures. Our interpretation assumes that the *illness* rate does not show any great variation between streams. The alternative explanation would postulate that boys who are ill frequently will tend to have a lower academic achievement, and thus be demoted more often than other boys. By the fourth year, therefore, the lower streams will contain a disproportionate number of boys who are subject

49

TABLE II

Absence Rates 1964-5

Form	Autumn Term	Spring Term
4A	2·79	6·28
4B	5·18	7·67
4C	7·36	12·82
4D	16·50	16·91

This absence rate is the number of absences as a percentage of maximum number of possible times present.

to frequent absence due to sickness. It is impossible to ascertain whether or not boys in lower streams are more often genuinely ill than boys in higher streams. But it is true, as the figures in Table III show, that there is some association between high absence and low achievement, and thus between absence and demotion. This table may imply that boys who are subject to frequent illness *or* that boys who truant frequently will tend to decline in stream. We have no means of verifying which of these two alternatives is correct. Perhaps it is a combination of both. Our data given in Chapter Two on the cases of truancy in lower streams, combined with the lack of informal pressure towards regular attendance, suggest that it is truants who tend to collect in lower streams – but there is no means by which we may prove that the differential absence rates do not mask differential illness rates.

One would expect a similar trend to show itself in the proportion of boys from each stream arriving late at school. The figures in Table IV support the prediction that the A stream has the lowest index of lateness, but there is no evidence of the predicted trend among the B, C and D streams. The figures represent all twenty forms at Lumley, since the figures for the fourth year alone are very small. We should also note that the figures are considerably less reliable than absence rates, since we note that many of the high status 4C and 4D boys often threatened prefects on late duty and thus avoided apprehension.

TABLE III

Absence and Achievement

| | | ACHIEVEMENT | | |
		High	*Medium*	*Low*
ABSENCE	*Low*	48	42	18
	Medium	30	44	43
	High	30	31	52

N = 338 boys

Chi-square = 25·78   D.f. = 4   P<0·01

These data are based on the 1st to 3rd year pupils 1963–4. High, medium and low refer to the upper, middle and lower thirds of absence rate and examination results for each separate form.

TABLE IV

Lates (Autumn Term 1964)

Stream	*Av. Number Lates per Boy*
A	0·18
B	0·58
C	0·49
D	0·48
E	1·14
All	0·53

The interpretation of the absence rate differentials was not unambiguous. A search for more 'pure' indices of differential commitment becomes essential. Perhaps the simplest would be an estimate of the degree of enjoyment of life at school – an educational equivalent of the industrial 'job satisfaction'. Accordingly, the boys were asked whether they liked or disliked school on the whole (Q.5). The distribution of replies is given in Table V. The degree of satisfaction with life at school falls as we move from the A to the D stream, and the results are statistically significant.*

TABLE V

Like/Dislike School

Form	% Like	% Dislike	N
4A	90	10	30
4B	75	25	28
4C	73	27	22
4D	52	48	23
All	74	26	103

Chi-square $= 9 \cdot 67$ D.f. $= 3$ $<$P$\cdot$025

A similar but more sharp differentiation of streams occurs in Table VI where the results to the question of whether the boys would like to leave school at the end of the Autumn Term 1964, that is, before reaching the age of fifteen years (Q.6). Here, the results, would occur by chance less than one in a thousand times. The boys of 4A are far more committed to school on this measure than any of the other forms.

A final question in this area asked whether or not the boys intended to take any further education after leaving school (Q.9). The results given in Table VII are perfectly in line with our prediction.

* p$<$·025, i.e. the results will occur by chance less than once in forty times.

TABLE VI

Leave/Stay at School

Form	% Leave	% Stay	N
4A	28	72	29
4B	71	29	28
4C	74	26	23
4D	70	30	23
All	59	41	103

Chi-square = 16·82   D.f. = 3   P < ·001

TABLE VII

Further Education

Form	% Yes	% No	N
4A	90	10	30
4B	68	32	28
4C	55	45	22
4D	32	68	22
All	64	36	102

Chi-square = 22·30   D.f. = 3   P < ·001

We may conclude that on the basis of the recorded absence rates, and on attitude questionnaires, the higher the stream, the greater the degree of commitment to school.

The best criteria are to be found in behavioural terms, that is, in the degree of participation of boys in school activities. Unfortunately there were no school societies at Lumley; however, we may derive some estimate from the participation in the school Football and Rugby teams, and in the school band and choir. The percentages of boys participating regularly (i.e. for at least one-third of all matches) in the football and rugby teams were 43 per cent, 27 per cent, 17 per cent, 22 per cent and 8 per cent for all boys in the A,B,C,D and E streams respectively. Though there is a reversal of the usual order in the case of the C and D streams, the predicted decline in degree of participation with stream recurs. The same trend appears when we consider the number of boys involved in the school choir, which performed at the Carol Service and at Concerts, and in the brass band. Musical activities are almost exclusively dominated by boys from the A and B streams: of the 61 boys concerned only two boys represent the whole of the C,D and E streams.

Two further indicators may be considered. Every week the boys were asked to contribute a few coppers to the School Fund, which was devoted to buying various kinds of equipment not supplied to the school by the local Authority and to the bulk purchase of athletic clothing, which was then resold to the boys at prices lower than these in local shops. The Headmaster announced the contributions from each form in Assembly on Monday mornings. When the average contributions per boy of the various streams are calculated, as in Table VIII, the usual trend appears.

TABLE VIII

School Fund and House Points (Autumn Term 1964)

Form	Mean contribution per boy (shillings)	Mean House points per boy	N
4A	2·3	49·1	30
4B	2·1	45·3	28
4C	1·1	116·3	23
4D	1·8	86·0	23

The second indicator, also presented in Table VIII, concerns the average number of House points per boy in each stream. House points were given at the discretion of individual teachers for good work or behaviour. Poor work or conduct was penalized by the deduction of House points. The Headmaster also awarded House points for high academic achievement in the terminal examinations, good attendance records, sporting successes and so on. The figures, however, show a reversal of the trends we have observed hitherto. To explain these figures we must remember that the House points were used by teachers as rewards. Since the teachers of the A and B, and the C and D, streams in the fourth year were often the same person for the same subject, we can consider the four streams in two pairs. In each case, the higher of the two streams has the better average. The reason for the higher averages in the C and D streams is accounted for by the greater liberality of their teachers in awarding House points. It seems reasonable to suppose that teachers of lower streams felt a greater need than teachers of higher streams to use the House points as incentives to good work and behaviour. The same reasoning accounts for the fact that the average for the E stream is greater than any other, namely 178·9. The E stream was in the main taught by one specialized teacher who taught none of the other fourth year forms.

It was suggested in Chapter Two that the norms of the A stream were in support of high standards of behaviour and dress, in conformity with the standards expected by teachers. In the lower streams, the group norms imposed standards of dress and behaviour which tended to deviate from those of the teachers: their long hair styles and jeans were strongly deplored and opposed by most of the teachers, and their 'messing' norm undermined the academic and disciplinary goals of the teachers. It seemed clear to the observer that the norms were accurately reflected in observable behaviour. Any visitor to the school would judge the dress and behaviour of upper stream boys as 'superior'. Such variations are, however, not easy to measure. The teachers completed questionnaires on the subject of the behaviour and appearance of each boy: 'behaviour' referred to the *general* classroom behaviour of each boy and 'appearance' included personal hygiene and dress. Each boy was rated on a five-point scale, ranging from Excellent (5), to Very Poor (1), with Average as the central score (3). One of the difficulties of such rating scales is the definition of 'average'. The raters were instructed to regard the term 'average' as being the average for the whole fourth year, not for any individual stream, though it is doubtful whether all the teachers followed this guide. The results for behaviour are presented in Table IX. The expected trend is fulfilled, though the differences between streams are very small: the difference between 4B and 4C is a mere ·01 of a point. But the reader should note that *individual* teachers are by no means agreed that behaviour is stream related.

TABLE IX

Teachers' Estimates of Pupils' Behaviour

Teacher	A	B	C	D	*All*
A	4·06	3·32	—	—	3·72
B	3·63	3·50	3·68	3·33	3·54
C	—	—	3·40	3·34	3·37
D	4·20	4·03	3·29	3·38	3·76
E	3·37	3·39	3·75	2·09	3·32
F	4·60	4·00	3·87	3·72	4·07
G	3·66	3·57	2·96	2·96	3·32
H	4·20	3·23	4·00	2·73	3·63
I	3·63	3·61	3·67	3·42	3·58
J	3·97	3·44	—	—	3·71
K	—	—	3·43	2·92	3·15
All Teachers	3·92	3·57	3·56	3·24	3·58

In Table X, which gives the results for the scores on appearance, the differentiation between stream is more marked, and individual teachers see appearance as much more stream-related than behaviour.

TABLE X

Teachers' Estimates of Pupils' Appearance

Teacher	A	B	C	D	*All*
A	3·93	3·29	—	—	3·62
B	3·50	3·25	3·18	2·62	3·16
C	—	—	3·21	3·08	3·15
D	4·63	3·93	3·25	2·96	3·75
E	3·33	3·14	3·31	2·08	3·15
F	4·33	3·89	3·25	2·75	3·61
G	4·17	3·28	3·54	2·79	3·25
H	4·33	3·61	3·40	2·86	3·61
I	4·23	3·89	3·37	3·21	3·72
J	3·97	3·18	—	—	3·59
K	—	—	3·14	3·08	3·11
All Teachers	4·05	3·49	3·18	2·91	3·44

We may consider these results in another way. Tables XI and XII divide the boys' scores into those which fall above and below the median. The figures clearly show the stream-related nature of both behaviour and appearance. Though both dimensions prove to be statistically significant, appearance differentiation is considerably sharper. We may thus conclude that our observations of actual dress and behaviour, and the normative structure of each form, are confirmed by teacher ratings: the higher the stream, the better the behaviour and appearance of the boys by teacher standards.

TABLE XI

Behaviour Scores

Form	Above Median	Below Median	N
4A	21	9	30
4B	17	11	28
4C	8	14	22
4D	5	17	22
All	51	51	102

Chi-square $= 14 \cdot 27$ D.f. $= 3$ P $< \cdot 005$

TABLE XII

Appearance Score

Form	Above Median	Below Median	N
4A	26	4	30
4B	17	11	28
4C	6	16	22
4D	3	19	22
All	52	50	102

Chi-square $= 33 \cdot 59$ D.f. $= 3$ P $< \cdot 001$

The evidence we have examined so far lends support to our analysis of the normative structure of each form as described in Chapter Two but there remains a number of areas for which little verification has been supplied. Accordingly, at the end of the Spring Term all the fourth year boys were asked to complete a multiple-choice questionnaire. That is, the major areas of the values discussed previously were converted into statements, with which each boy signified his agreement, disagreement or uncertainty.[2]

One of the many flaws affecting such tests is that boys may choose one of the three answers which does not correspond to his real attitude. We have good grounds for suspecting that some boys, especially those in the lower streams, might treat the test as an amusing situation and deceive the tester with random or misleading answers. To check this tendency the test included a number of statements where on *a priori* grounds the answer can be predicted. An example of such a statement (Q.10 viii) is, 'I like a teacher who can take a joke and have a laugh with the lads.' There is no reason to assume that any boy should disagree with this view, since even those boys who are at the extremes of the academic or anti-academic dimension should agree with this statement. The check questions all produced satisfactory results: only in very rare cases did a boy respond against the expected direction – in our example, one boy disagreed. Despite this, the writer is certain that some of the high status boys from the lower streams responded in ways which conformed to teacher rather than their own ideals. The extent of this trend is impossible to assess.

The details of the results to this 'Orientation Test' are given in Table XIII with the trends in streams and the levels of probability. Although significant differences between the streams were not found on some questions, for example long hair, the major areas of normative differentiation suggested in Chapter Two receive support. We may summarize the results in the generalization that the higher the stream, the more likely its members will approve of:

—boys who work hard in lessons.

—boys who do not copy.

—boys who do not have fun in lessons.

—boys who pay attention in lessons.

—boys who obey teachers.

—boys who are polite to teachers.

—boys who have good manners.

—teachers who control the class and keep the boys quiet.

—teachers who make the boys work hard.

—teachers who punish boys who misbehave in lessons.

—boys who do not wear jeans at school.

—boys who do not have long hair at school.

—boys who attend regularly.

—boys who do not smoke.

—boys who have interesting hobbies.

In all these cases there is a statistically significant tendency for boys in the lower streams to hold the reverse opinion.

A second way in which we may assess the differences between streams is to score the answers and then make comparisons between streams. It can readily be seen that all the items of the test are, as the title suggests, a measure of conformity towards the values approved by the school system and the teachers. Each question thus contains a continuum with two extremes, agree and disagree, and a central area of uncertainty. In the scoring system, the opinion closest to that approved by teachers is given three marks, the 'uncertain' answer two marks, and the opinion furthest from teacher approval one mark. The higher the score, the greater will be the tendency towards holding values and attitudes approved by teachers. The result of the analysis are given in Table XIV. The average score of 4A boys is far higher than any of the other three streams, which, though falling in the expected direction, cluster closely together.

TABLE XIII

Orientation Test Items

Item	chi-square	P
Academic 1. Boys who work hard	23·31	<·001

Item	chi-square	P
2. Boys who do not allow copying	13·05	<·005
3. Boys who do not have fun in lessons	8·94	<·05
4. Boys who pay attention in class	19·16	<·001
5. Boys who obey teachers	14·45	<·005
6. Boys who are not cheeky to teachers	11·74	<·01
7. Boys who are willing to help teachers	2·98	N.S.
8. Teachers who control the class	8·43	<·05
9. Teachers who make boys work	18·69	<·001
10. Teachers who punish 'messers'	7·99	<·05
Appearance 11. Boys should not be allowed to wear jeans at school	13·40	<·005
12. Boys should not be allowed to have long hair at school	5·44	N.S.
13. Boys who do not have long hair	14·71	<·005
14. Boys who are clean and tidy	8·18	N.S.
General Commitment to School 15. Boys should not be allowed to leave school at 14 years	26·10	<·001
16. Boys who attend regularly	13·72	<·005
17. Boys who do not come late	3·03	N.S.
18. Boys who do not smoke	12·85	<·005
19. Boys should not be allowed to smoke in school	10·39	<·025

Item	chi-square	P
20. Boys who play sports	4·60	N.S.
21. Boys who respect the school	7·25	N.S.
22. Boys should wear a school uniform	1·34	N.S.
23. Boys with an interesting hobby	20·04	<·001
24. Boys who are not good fighters	4·84	N.S.
*25. Boys who are prefects	5·38	N.S.
*26. Boys who are teachers' pets	2·08	N.S.
27. Boys who have good manners	12·14	<·01
*28. Boys who come from a nice home	3·05	N.S.

*not included in the test scoring.

Note: Items are presented in the pro-school (score 3) form. The actual items are given in Appendix III Q.10. Where p<·05 the association is between high stream and pro-school responses. In each case d.f. = 3, since the 'uncertain' responses have been combined with the smaller of the agree/disagree columns.

TABLE XIV
Orientation Test Scores

Form	Mean Score	Above Median	Below Median	N
4A	63·83	27	3	30
4B	54·28	16	12	28
4C	52·59	7	15	22
4D	50·23	6	16	22
All	55·85	50	52	102

Chi-square = 26·50   D.f. = 3   P<·001.

A guide to the association of high orientation to school and high stream can be seen in the numbers of boys in each form whose scores fall above or below the median of the fourth year as a whole. This distribution would occur by chance less than once in a thousand times. We may conclude that the numerous indices discussed in this chapter confirm the analysis of the normative structure of each of the four forms.

Central to this analysis was the suggestion that not only do the norms become increasingly anti-academic as we move down the streams, but also that in the A stream the high status boys are more orientated to the school than the low status boys, and the reverse in the B,C and D streams. Table XV gives the average scores for the high and low status boys in each form. The difference between the two halves in 4A is small, but in the expected direction. In the other three forms the relation between status and orientation to school is confirmed. Table XVI presents some individual items of the test analysed in terms of form and status level.

TABLE XV

Informal Status and Orientation Score

Form	Mean Score	
	High Status	Low Status
4A	64·19	63·46
4B	49·72	58·86
4C	49·45	55·73
4D	47·19	53·27

Of the many advantages of statistical analysis, one of the most striking is the condensation of a multiplicity of facts into a few figures. Correlation is a tool which enables us to indicate by a single number the extent to which two different aspects or variables are associated with each other.*

In describing the values of each form, we have shown that the leaders, those boys who exercise the most influence in the form, are those boys who examplify and enforce the norms.[3] If this is true, we should expect the correlations between informal status ranks and other measures to give significant correlations. For example, it should be true in the higher streams that informal status and academic position will correlate positively, but in the lower streams a negative correlation would be predicted. Table XVII lists the correlations between our major variables. The correlations between informal status and academic position are in the predicted direction. There is a significant positive correlation for 4A but this declines sharply to a low correlation for 4B. In 4C and 4D there is a low negative correlation, not the high negative correlation which we would expect. The main reason for this result lies in the tendency of the high status boys in this form to occupy central positions in the academic hierarchy, since as we have seen they controlled their academic positions to avoid very high and very low positions, both of which bore risks of promotion or demotion.

From our previous discussion one would predict a high positive correlation between informal status and behaviour in 4A, a high negative correlation in 4C and 4D, and an intermediate coefficient for 4B. The results confirm the prediction, especially for 4C and 4D.[4] The correlation for 4B is slightly negative, which is in line with the tendency for the higher status boys to be non-academic in their orientation. But the correlation of $+ \cdot 18$ for 4A is surprisingly low. The explanation for this is twofold. Firstly, we must remember that it was the B clique,

---

* In correlation, where the ranks on our indices are exactly the same on both variables, the correlation is perfect and has a coefficient of $+1$; where the top rank on one variable is bottom on the other and so on, the correlation is *negative*, with a coefficient of -1; when the coefficient is o, the degree of association is inconsistent or random. Coefficients of correlation fall somewhere between $+1$ and -1, and only in very rare cases at the two extremes. The most usual method of calculating rank correlation is that provided by Spearman's *rho*, but since our variables include ties, that is cases where two or more boys occupy the same rank, we shall use Kendall's *tau*, which is method that can take account of such ties. But we must remember that as a rule the coefficient of correlation produced by Kendall's *tau* is lower than that by Spearman's *rho*. For example, the correlation between informal status and academic position in 4A is $+ \cdot 69$ by Spearman's *rho*, but $+ \cdot 50$ by Kendall's *tau*.

TABLE XVI

Orientation Test Items by Form and Status

	4A		4B		4C		4D	
	High	*Low*	*High*	*Low*	*High*	*Low*	*High*	*Low*
Like boy who gets on with work	93	93	43	64	9	55	36	55
Dislike teachers who make boys work hard	0	20	50	21	73	36	73	55
Dislike boys who let you copy	80	73	14	64	18	55	36	36
Like boys you can have a lot of fun with in lessons	47	40	71	36	73	64	100	55
Dislike boy who is cheeky to teachers	87	87	29	93	27	73	36	55
Like teachers who punish messers	87	60	43	50	45	55	18	55
Boys should be allowed to wear jeans in school (agree)	33	47	57	50	100	45	91	82
Boys should not be allowed to smoke in school	87	87	29	64	36	64	45	55

All figures are percentages.

not the A clique, which was the 'intellectual' group in the form, and secondly, the newcomers in the form tended to score very highly on behaviour, despite low status. If we exclude the new-comer to 4A from the calculation, the correlation between informal status and behaviour rises from $+\cdot18$ to $+\cdot30$ which is closer to the predicted level.

The correlation between informal status and appearance are in the expected direction: in the A stream, the high status boys tend

TABLE XVII

Rank Correlations

Variables	4A	4B	4C	4D
Informal Status–Academic Position	+·50*	+·16	—·15	—·15
Informal Status–Behaviour	+·18	—·12	—·58*	—·57*
Informal Status–Appearance	+·37*	—·31*	—·41*	—·21
Behaviour–Appearance	+·44*	+·60*	+·56*	+·52*
Behaviour–Academic Position	+·26*	+·21	+·48*	+·15
Orientation–Behaviour	+·22	+·33*	+·44*	+·24
Informal Status–Orientation	+·07	—·49*	—·40*	—·35*

All coefficients by Kendall's tau.
*Statistically significant.

to dress well, but the reverse is true for the lower streams. The significant positive correlations between behaviour and appearance for all forms agree with our observations – that those who deviate from the school's behavioural expectations are those who tend to wear jeans and long hair. But it is important to note that they may reflect the bias of teachers as raters by producing a so-called 'halo effect', whereby the raters tend to ascribe a whole set of favourable scores or unfavourable scores to any one subject. That is, there is a tendency for judges to perceive a subject as either generally 'good' or generally 'bad' and rate him accordingly.

The positive correlations between behaviour and orientation, and between behaviour and academic position are in the expected positive direction for all forms. Since the Orientation Test is really a measure of the level of general conformity to school values, we should expect it to correlate highly with informal status in 4A, less so in 4B, and negatively in 4C and 4D. The results confirm our prediction for 4C and 4D, but the coefficient for 4B is more negative, and for 4A less positive, than predicted. However, if we exclude the newcomers to 4A from our calculations, the positive correlation between informal status and orientation rises from $+ \cdot 07$ to $+ \cdot 32$.

In two of the correlations for 4A we have noted that the results are closer to the predicted level if the newcomers are excluded. For the correlations between informal status and behaviour, and informal status and orientation, are more positive if we consider the 4A core members alone. All the newcomers had low status in the form, but only two of them were highly deviant. The remaining seven newcomers show signs of *over-conformity* to the school's values and some of the 4A norms. For example, the average orientation test score for 4A is 63·83, but for these seven newcomers the average score is 66·29; similarly, the average behaviour score for 4A is 3·92, but for these seven newcomers it is 4·25. The newcomers in 4A are more conformist to school values than any other group, including high status 4A boys.

Our attempt to measure the values in different streams suggested in earlier observation and analysis has been broadly successful. The results lead to the generalization that the higher the stream, the greater the extent of pupil commitment to school, satisfaction with school life, and conformity to the expectations of the teachers. Boys in low streams tend to be the reverse of high stream pupils in these respects. Secondly, our analysis of normative differences *within* streams has been broadly substantiated: the higher the stream the greater is the tendency for high status to be associated with attitudes, values and behaviour expected by the school; in low streams, high status is negatively associated with conformity to school expectations.

Chapter Four

RELATIONS BETWEEN STREAMS

The fourth year forms at Lumley School are not the separate entities we have tended to assume in our discussion. Whilst it is true that each form spent the major portion of the school day as a teaching unit, the social world of any one boy was not limited to teachers and classmates. The results of the friendship choices given in Table I show that between twenty and forty per cent of choices are directed to boys in different streams. But this is a minority. The organization of the school imposes severe limitations on opportunities for interaction between boys from different streams, and is thus a major factor influencing the formation of friendships. Now that we have examined the norms or values and the prestige hierarchies in different streams, we must relate our observations to the way in which members of different streams perceive one another.

When the boys were asked to name the boy they disliked most in the whole fourth year (Q.7), we find that the lower streams frequently name Adrian and the higher streams frequently name Clint. These two boys act as a focus of the conflict between the values of these groups. The purpose of this chapter will be to show that there is an intimate connection between a form's values and its members' perception of other forms.

Our understanding of this relation can be confirmed and enlarged by an examination of the relevant items of the Sentence Completion Test. This test is designed to elicit information about a subject's attitude towards and perception of a given phenomenon. It consists of a series of incomplete sentences which the subject is asked to finish. It is thus an 'open-ended' test, which does not require the subject to select from a group of predetermined answers. The assumption is that the content of the

68

completion of the sentence will disclose the subject's attitude. Naturally this test is not a standardized one. The answers can be difficult to interpret and unless consistent or reliable methods of scoring are devised, the interpretation of responses may become dangerously subjective.*

Among the items in the Sentence Completion Test administered to all the boys in the fourth year were:

The boys in 4A are . . .

The boys in 4D are . . .

All the responses to these items were assigned to one of three categories, positive, negative and neutral. A residual category, unclassifiable, contains those responses which are ambiguous or difficult to interpret and omissions.

The positive category includes all responses which are considered to be favourable to the form. Examples of this category are:

. . . great.

. . . all good to get on with.

. . . more intelligent than others.

. . . the best bunch of lads anyone could hope to meet.

. . . smashing 'cos they join in our life.

The negative category includes those responses which are considered unfavourable to the form in question.

. . . all snobs.

. . . a load of bigheads.

. . . puffs.

. . . soft, teachers pets all of them.

. . . bent, mad, scruffy.

The responses which contain a favourable and an unfavourable comment, or which qualify the first comment, are assigned to the neutral category.

. . . alright until they start getting noisy and mess about in class.

* In this test, once the criteria had been established, the agreement between judges was 97 per cent for the fourth year forms, and with a different second judge 98 per cent for the second year forms.

. . . on the whole alright, but there are some that don't fit in.

. . . a good lot. Some bigheads though.

. . . good lads but some are soft.

. . . Great. Others are twits.

. . . some are alright, but others are messers.

The omissions or indeterminate responses account for some 4 per cent of the total number of responses made.

The results of the categorization of the responses to these two items on the test are given below in Tables XVIII and XIX. They can be subsumed under the generalization that the greater the distance between two streams, the more negative the attitudes these streams will hold towards each other. Of particular interest are the comments of the A and D streams about each other, since it is these two forms which form the extremes of separation. 4A's comments about 4D include:

. . . thick, most of them.

. . . the rough type, a bad type.

. . . mostly scruffy.

. . . mixed up trouble makers.

. . . not willing to learning anything.

. . . a waste of school time and not willing to learn anything.

. . . just lower the reputation of the school.

. . . bullies and think they're tough.

. . . dirty disgusting layabouts.

This antipathy was fully reciprocated by 4D's comments on 4A.

. . . a load of soft nigs.

. . . are treated like angels and us like louts.

. . . a load of sisis.

. . . brainey showoff and they all go to the fire station and never us.

. . . bigheads they think they know everything.

. . . too posh.

These responses exemplify not only the hostility that exists between the extremes of the streaming system, but also the basis on which these boys make value-judgements about one another. This basis consists of the dominant norms current in that form, as illustrated in the previous chapter. Boys in 4A condemn boys in 4D for being unintelligent, academically lazy, 'messers', aggressive and untidy since the reverse of these qualities is normative in 4A and non-conformists within 4A are rejected. Conversely, boys in 4D despise 4A boys for being academically orientated, hard-working, teachers' favourites, 'posh', and cowardly since it is through display of the reverse of these qualities that informal status is achieved. Both 4A and 4D can term each other 'bigheads': the definition of the term is relative to the dominant group norms.

TABLE XVIII

Boys in 4A are . . .

Form	% Positive	% Neutral	% Negative	% Not classified	N
4A	63	30	7	—	30
4B	21	32	46	—	28
4C	25	21	46	8	24
4D	14	14	68	4	22
All	33	25	39	3	104

Chi-square = 27·65   D.f. = 6   P < ·001

By the fourth year the boys at Lumley School have developed stereotypes about the kind of boy to be expected at the extremes of the streaming system. We must call them stereotypes, since the judgements are made less on the basis of actual interaction – Table I shows how rare it is for boys from 4A and 4D to become friends – than in terms of the general values they know to be current in that particular form, these values tending to be the reverse of their own. The negative attitudes are disseminated with little direct or extended interaction. The stereotyped nature

TABLE XIX

Boys in 4D are . . .

Form	% Positive	% Neutral	% Negative	% Not classified	N
4A	10	27	60	3	30
4B	7	32	46	14	28
4C	46	21	33	—	24
4D	73	9	14	5	22
All	31	23	39	6	104

Chi-square = 33·77   D.f. = 6   P<·001

of inter-stream perception is clear from the results to the 'dislike' question (Q.3). Eighteen of the twenty dislike choices from 4A and 4B to 4C are directed at Clint; twelve of the fourteen dislikes given by 4C and 4D to 4A are directed at Adrian. Clint, as 'cock' of the school, and Adrian, as school captain, are well known and highly visible as leaders of their groups. They become representatives of their groups, embodiments of the values they support, and thus targets to their opponents.

The data discussed so far in this section were collected in order to allow some measurement to be made, to demonstrate that the processes being described are not due to the mis-perceptions of the observer, but to real statistically significant differences. In this way the reader is provided with a dry, static table in which the fluid and dynamic social process is fixed. We must in part destroy the specimen to view it under the microscope. Data collected by means of questionnaires sacrifice depth and quality to brevity and quantitative assessment. It is through extracts from discussions with the boys that our appreciation can be heightened.

When boys from any form, but especially those from 4A or 4D, discussed inter-stream relations, they frequently confessed to simply *not knowing* members of that form. What they did say confirms our findings. They are stereotyped attitudes based on hearsay or superficial observation rather than on personal experience of one another. Despite the frequent accuracy in terms of the high status members, these perceptions are generalized to cover all members of the form, and the comments reveal the depth of the mutual fear and distrust. Consider the comments of boys in 4A and 4B on members of the C and D streams.

Most of them are bullies, aren't they?

They're scruffy. They get good clothes but they don't look after them.

In 4C they're all hard. And they mess about.

We never sort of mix with them.

They're teddy boys. They think they're tough.

A few of them are all right in 4C. A lot of them are bigheaded, you know, walking round beating kids up and smoking.

They dress different and they're always pushing people around and all that.

They all *look* dumb.

I'd rather be in 4A than in 4C. They're always messing about hitting you and all that. Like Clint. He's in that class. I don't fancy that.

(4B boy)

I'd rather be bottom of the top class than top of the bottom class.

(4B boy)

It was in discussion about Clint that the fear and antipathy of A and B boys expressed itself most clearly.

He [Clint] acts big. Like when he goes in the prefects' corner. He won't go and you can't throw him out. They all say, 'Why don't you throw him out?' but you can't.

(Adrian)

It's just his act you know. He gets a bad name in the class you know. He's always having to go to [the Head] for the stick. Being caned for smoking and things like that. And he's always threatening little kids. People are afraid of you if you

73

go swaggering about the playground threatening everybody.

I'm not really frightened of him. I just don't go near him. He's not so tough on his own but there's a big gang of his.

I'd run if he threatened to smash me. It'd be no use if you beat him up 'cos he'd get you with his gang some time. I've never seen him fight but they say he fought one of the prefects last year.

4C's the worst class 'cos Clint's in that.

I'm frightened of Clint. They all talk about him and say he's a belting scrapper.

All Clint's gang are good fighters. If you get someone who mucks around with Clint, but isn't really a good fighter, and you start messing with him, you know, then he gets Clint on to you. You can't do nowt against his crowd.

I'm glad some of the people who did go down went down, 'cos all the people who used to go around with Clint, well if they start pushing you about, you can't hit them, or three kids'll come up and set on you or summat like that. You see you can't touch them. But now you've got no worry about that, 'cos they're not in our class any more.

They're all bigheads in 4C. Clint and all them lot. They pick on you.

The general trend was thus for the members of the A and B streams to ignore the C and D boys. This is as much the result of fear of physical aggression as of the difference in values. They followed a policy of disarming the enemy, who was only too anxious to be provoked into a demonstration of his 'toughness', by forgetting his existence.

The C and D boys were not in a position to ignore the A and B boys so easily, since it was predominantly from these upper streams that the school prefects and teams were drawn. Moreover the Headmaster was frequently able to bring them to public attention by his eulogies of their achievements and good behaviour. It is not easy for inferiors to ignore superiors, for failures to take no account of publicly acknowledged successes. To be so scornfully ignored by the A and B boys increased the

C and D boys' sense of inferiority. It was a common source of complaint.

They don't speak to you or owt in 4A.

They just don't let on to you. They just look at you, you know. Just 'cos they're in a higher class. I feel like smashing them sometimes.

They snub you and all that. You know, they just walk right past you.

They're snobby in 4A. There are some lads who used to go to our [Junior] School but now they're up there they don't look at you.

I don't like that Adrian. If you let on to him he'll snub you.

There are a lot of snobby ones that won't talk to you. You know, Adrian and all them. They're in a high class and they think they can boss everyone around. If you walk past them and say summat they just ignore you.

In their comments on the members of the A and B streams the boys from 4C and 4D demonstrate the incompatibility of the norms dominant in the upper and lower streams.

They're all daft. Toffee-noses. You know, snobs. They think they're clever. They're bound to be clever at the top, aren't they?

Some are all right. But you know some of them think they're it just because they're taking the exam. They don't want to know you. You know, they make you feel sort of out of place.

Just 'cos they're in a higher class than us they think they're *better* than us. They are in a way, but they don't need to stick their necks out do they?

I don't like 4A. They're a class who've got to get on with their work. They've no time to mess about. They just do the work.

It's the way they act. It's them little brief cases. Just 'cos they've got them they think they're Lord Muck.

They're teachers' pets. in 4A. Like Adrian. He gets on my

nerves. He tries to throw you out [of school] and that. He told me he was going to get the teachers to throw me out – but he wouldn't do it himself. They change when they become prefects.

Adrian and Arnold and that lot. They're always hanging around the teachers and that. That's soft.

They're all mad that lot. They're all staying on most of them. They must like school if they're staying on.

In between 4C and 4D, you know, they're the same. But them above 4C are clever. They come to school with their uniform and tie. They've gone worse since they came here. You know they used to be just like us, you know, mess about and everything. And untidy and that.

The people who're cleverer than us, the lads who're in 4A and that, well, they come to school in ties and that and they're posh to us. They don't talk to us, you know what I mean?

Some are snobby just 'cos you smoke and that. They don't want to have anything to do with you. They don't seem to think their mothers and fathers smoke.

I just don't like them getting treated better than us, you know what I mean? [The teachers] call them by their first names and they just treat us as though we're not there.

The school-orientated behaviour of the A (and some of the B) boys, which contravenes the dominant norms of the lower two streams, thus becomes a target of criticism, which is frequently summarized or stereotyped into a charge of being 'posh' or 'snobby' or 'teachers' pets', or attacks upon the symbols of their superiority, such as their brief-cases or the person of Adrian. The pressures existing in the lower streams against the patterns of behaviour current in the higher streams are evident in the answers I received to the question: What would it be like if the Headmaster suddenly transferred you to 4A?

If I was put in 4A I'd refuse to go. I'd put in for a transfer to another school.

I'd feel daft in that class with them. I don't want to start speaking like them. They think I'm dumb just 'cos they're in a higher class.

They'd all say, 'Look at him, he's going in 4A.' And I don't want to come in a tie. They all wear them and I can't be the odd one out.

I wouldn't go in. I'd stay off. I don't like them from what I've heard of it. All my mates would call me snobby and that.

You see if anyone goes up all the lads in 4D think that you're like better than them, snobby, you know. And that's how you lose all your mates. *I'd rather stay a dunce and have friends than be a genius without friends.*

These facts may be analysed in terms of *reference groups*, which is a term used by social psychologists to refer to those groups to which a person relates himself. When the reference group is *positive*, the person either aspires to be a member of the group or evaluates himself in terms of the group; when the reference group is *negative*, the person does not wish to be a member or evaluates himself in terms opposed to the values of the group. In this sense we can regard the A and D streams' perception of each other as negative reference groups.

A stream boys evaluate themselves and one another in terms of conformity to their dominant values, and thus do not aspire to membership of the D stream. Likewise D stream boys regard A stream membership and values negatively. Whilst with A stream boys this desire to remain in the same 'top' form will act as an incentive towards academic achievement, the reverse will be true for low stream boys. The informal pressures within the low streams tend to work directly against the assumption of the teachers that boys will regard promotion into a higher stream as a desirable goal. The boys from the low streams were very reluctant to ascend into higher streams because their stereotypes of A and B stream boys were defined in terms of values alien to their own and because promotion would involve rejection by their low stream friends. The teachers were not fully aware that this unwillingness to be promoted to a higher stream led the high informal status boys to depress their performance in examinations. This fear of promotion adds to our list of factors leading to the formation of anti-academic attitudes in low stream boys.

> I didn't want to be top of the class. I wanted to stay where I was. That's why I stayed off [school] for the test. But I had to do them when I came back and I was top so I have to move up.

It has been suggested that one of the reasons for the hostility between streams is that the organization of the streams led to an increased isolation or reduced interaction between members of different streams, which led to growth of stereotyped attitudes and perceptions and normative differentiation. The stereotypes begin to disintegrate in those few activities where members from upper and lower streams were involved in an activity which required co-operation. Such a situation is provided by the school Rugby Team, which was organized and trained by the form teacher of 4D, who was most anxious to recruit members of his form. Regular members of the team comprised six boys from 4A, four from 4B and seven from 4D. The inevitable disunity first revealed itself in the selection of the captain.

> We all thought it would be 28 [from 4A]. He was giving orders and all that. And when he found out that I [Don of 4D] was captain he was real mad, 'cos he's been captain in second and third year.

After this it was hardly expected that inter-stream relations among team members would be cordial: form loyalties were more demanding than those of the team. Action needed to be taken if the team was to succeed.

> [4A boys] wouldn't pass to us. They keep it to theirselves. So we told Mr. ——. We said, 'Put us on one side and them on the other, so we can have it out with them' – you know what I mean? So he let us do that.

> When we first went for Rugby practice, they wouldn't pass to us. So we got on the opposite team. And we banged 'em hard and all that. We tripped 'em up and all that, you see what I mean? But when we got on the team and got to see how one another played, they passed it about. They thought we were not as good as them, but they don't think that now.

The more these boys interacted in a co-operative activity, the less easily they were able to maintain their stereotypes. The feelings of dislike slowly yielded to acceptance.

> 28's all right. He's on the Rugger Team.

Joint membership of a team was one of the very few bases on which 4A or 4D boys would express approval of one another.

So far our discussion has been concerned with the relations between the upper and lower streams, between A/B and C/D. There was little hostility between 4C and 4D, since we have seen that the high status boys in these two forms were strongly inter-linked by friendship choices. Between 4A and 4B, as indicated in Chapter Two, relations were not so cordial: the norms of the high status boys in the upper streams were not similar. 4A had gained the most academically orientated members from 3B and lost its least academically orientated members to 4B. The values of 4B boys seem to form a compromise between the academic values of the A stream and the anti-academic values of the C and D streams. Whereas in the third year the A and B streams were involved in competition, by the fourth year the A stream members were thought of as boys who were intending to remain at school for a fifth year and the B stream as boys who intended to leave during the fourth year. 4A members thus tended to see themselves as academically superior to, and more hard-working than, 4B boys.

> They're a bit stupid in 4B. They're always messing about. They behave more like a second year than a fourth year. They don't take work seriously enough. They make excuses for not doing their homework. Alan and 09 are like that in our class.

> They muck about a lot in 4B. They do different things than us you know what I mean? You'd get nothing done with them. It's all right, you know, mucking about a bit, but they never stop really.

> In 4B they're a different lot altogether. In 4A they're all like sensible. In 4B they tend to muck about a bit, don't they?

> We're more sensible in 4A 'cos they're always mucking about in 4B.

We're more serious minded. They're always out for a laugh.

This perception of the B stream norms is fairly accurate, but because the dominant norms of the high status boys are generalized to cover *all* 4B members, there is evidence of stereotypy. We may observe a similar trend in the B boys' perception of A boys. Whilst it is true that the low status, academically orientated members of 4B showed virtually no signs of hostility –

We're much the same. There's not much difference between us.

– the high status 4B boys tend to describe 4A boys in terms of the stereotype developed by low stream boys.

They're snobby most of them in 4A. They're brainy and everything.

They wear ties in 4A 'cos they're toffs. They don't wear them 'cos they like them. You see, they used to get House points for them in second and third year.

They wear a different type of clothes. They all wear sports jackets and suits and they wear ties more than we would. I like an open collar.

We never get the Head Boy in our class.

They're mad in 4A, staying on at school. The boys who leave early get better jobs than them as stay on. Most of them do, anyway.

We don't like the lads in 4A. They're all right out of school but in school they're getting round the teachers, you know. I keep as far away from them as I can. [Other boys] get the teachers' pet outside.

Adrian and all them, they're bigheads. They show off all the time. They think they're dead brainy.

It would be different if we were in 4A. All the teachers are better with 4A. They're always saying 4A are better than us.

They think they're better than us in 4A. They're all teachers' pets.

I don't want to go up. I don't like them. I think they're snobs.

Some of them. I think some of them, Adrian and Arnold, think they're better than us. They think they're brainier just 'cos they're in a higher class than you. Just 'cos they're prefects, they think, 'I can push anyone around I like.'

I'd feel rotten if they moved me into that class 'cos I don't like them. Adrian and Arnold and that lot. And you can't have any fun in that class. They're all working. They don't mess about. But in our class they mess about and you can have some fun.

Some of the people are all right, but some of them are big-headed. Well, I think so anyway. I don't feel at home with them, you know. They all keep together and don't bother with you. There's always something wrong with you.

The competition which had existed between 3A and 3B during the previous academic year declined. Superiority in games, attendance, contributions to funds, House points and academic achievement are less a matter of rivalry between the two upper streams.

All the argument between the forms has died out. In the third year we used to decide things by football. We used to win usually. But if we got beat by them, they used to think it was marvellous. But now, we don't play now. Some of the boys who've gone down used to play football for us.

The only reason they get more than we do is that if they miss one week they have to pay a shilling and if they miss again it's another shilling. In our class if you miss it's fourpence the next week and then eightpence after that.

They try to beat us. They give sixpences and all that. But Mr. —— won't take more than twopence.

If they broke the record, we'd get it back.

(A boys)

There was some rivalry between us and 3A in soccer last year. But there's not much rivalry now.

There's some rivalry over the school fund.

If we all give two bob each to the Old Folks' thinggy, Mr.

────── will put ten bob to it. We'll win this, but we've not beaten their attendance.

We're pleased if we win the shield because we get off quarter of an hour early, but we're not all that bothered.

In maths it's like a battle between our class and their class. And how long you're off [from school], for this shield, you know. You know, it's all right if either 4A or 4B win it. But they say, We've got to beat 4A or we've got to beat 4B. Just like that.

(B boys)

In a word, it seems that the division of the upper streams into those who intended to take the C.S.E. and those who intended to leave during the fourth year erected a barrier between 4A and 4B, producing a differentiation of norms, reduction in rivalry and stereotyped hostile attitudes.

We may conclude that the streams exert a powerful influence on the extent and form of interaction between age-mates in the same neighbourhood school. Boys tend to interact with and choose friends from boys in the same stream and only rarely from streams more than one removed from their own. As the predominant norms of each form become differentiated and various barriers to communication between streams are erected, negative stereotypes develop. These serve to reinforce the normative differentiation and inhibit further cross-stream interaction, and thus the incentive value of the 'promotion' system is undermined for low stream boys.

Chapter Five

TEACHER-PUPIL
RELATIONS

Ninety per cent of the pupils at Lumley were born in the depressed industrial area in which the school is situated. They live and spend most of their leisure time there: it is 'home'. In contrast, only one of the teachers lives in the area, and a small minority lives inside the town boundaries. Most of the teachers live in the residential suburbs outside the town, where the grime and poverty are less apparent, and from which they travel to school each morning by car. Although many are natives of the town, and although some are working-class in origin, their educational experience tends to be that of a Grammar School and University or Training College. Their attitudes and values are naturally those of settled middle-class adults, whose lives are rooted in the town and its environs, but in a contrasting social setting to that of the pupils.

Much has been written by sociologists of the 'cultural clash' between teachers and working-class pupils. Mays, writing about schools in a similar area, stated:

> The teachers in the school find themselves at the nexus of two distinct cultures with a correspondingly difficult role to play. Being themselves mainly conditioned by the grammar school tradition and the middle-class system of values, they have to make a drastic mental readjustment to be able to deal sympathetically with the people whose attitudes and standards are so different. Even those teachers who have themselves risen from working-class backgrounds, do not, contrary to what is generally supposed, always find it psychologically an easy matter to adopt a sympathetic, uncondemnatory attitude towards the less favoured representatives of their own social class.[1]

From what has been said one would expect evidence of this 'cultural clash' at Lumley Secondary Modern school, and much of this chapter will be devoted to an analysis of the conflicts between teachers and pupils. Yet it is important to remember that a researcher is constantly in danger of selecting evidence which supports a particular argument, or highlights a particular aspect of the social system, but which excludes data which contribute to the formation of a more general pattern. Of course, research involves selection of material for analysis, but we must be concerned to fit it into the more general pattern.

The staff at Lumley was remarkably stable: there were no signs of the high rates of staff turnover which have been reported for schools in 'problem' areas. 85 per cent of the teachers during the academic year 1964-5 had been at the school at least as long as the fourth year pupils, whereas the equivalent percentage from the slum schools examined in the Newsom Report is 55 per cent. At Lumley no teachers had both joined and left the school staff within this period 1962-5, whereas the figure in the Newsom Report for similar schools is 37 per cent.[2] The reasons for this stability of staff at Lumley cannot be assessed here and the figures of themselves do not automatically imply that this stability was beneficial to the school. But it is clear that this very low turnover rate means that the boys in this school were not subjected to transient relationships with their teachers.

In many respects the relations between teachers and pupils in this school were friendly, sympathetic, co-operative and constructive. Most of the teachers were genuinely concerned about the lives, careers and prospects of the boys in their care, even of those boys whose attitudes and behaviour in school were antagonistic and rarely a source of teacher satisfaction. The lack of school societies at Lumley has already been indicated. This may to some extent reflect the lack of interest of the teachers in organizing such activities, and the lack of interest of the pupils in participating in them. It is certainly true that many boys had part-time jobs after school which would inhibit involvement in extra-curricular activities. Whilst some members of staff were indeed very anxious to quit school as soon as possible after the end of afternoon school, others were willing to supervise and encourage pupils in informal groups in the art rooms and workshops.

Moreover, a number of teachers supervised games on Saturday mornings; these people voluntarily travelled some distance to referee these games and gave up lunch breaks to train the teams. The school also had a fine history for organizing school holidays, in various parts of the British Isles and on the Continent. But some teachers took no part in any of these activities.

Many of the teachers were inevitably ambivalent about their jobs. From their professional training they derived ideals of what they were expected to achieve as teachers, but they were forced to deal with material which was frequently apathetic or intractable. They would thus tend to vary between feelings of depression and frustration when they considered their efforts to be without fruit or purpose, and moods of a more elated and jocular missionary confidence. Because the rewards were so small and intangible, it was the former mood which predominated, and teachers often blamed the home environment of the boys for many of their setbacks and failures as teachers. After a short period in the school most of the teachers had to make some kind of adjustment to the situation. It is this compromise with the products of a deprived area which we must now consider.

When I first arrived at Lumley School I was surprised by the informality of the relations between teachers and pupils. Since my own previous teaching experience had been acquired in a highly selective Grammar School of ancient foundation, this lack of formality was striking. The usual form of address to a teacher – 'sir' – was used much less frequently than in the grammar school, and the kind of remarks a boy would make to a teacher, and be accepted by the teacher, were less tinged with the 'politeness' and sense of social distance to which I had become accustomed. At first I suspected that some of the boys were being rather rude to me, until I discovered that this was their natural mode of communication to the staff. The tendencies for teachers to call boys by their first names, for boys to make personal remarks about the teachers' dress or car, for boys to walk into the staff room on various missions, all conflicted with my experience of the formal, masters-in-gowns, academic atmosphere of a grammar school. When the teachers learned that I had previously been in a grammar school, they commented:

Oh, you'll find things different here.

You've got to remember these kids haven't much ability.

You've struck the bottom of the barrel here.

The self-conscious acceptance of the school as a Secondary Modern in a poor area betrayed itself in a number of interesting ways. Only one member of staff, who came to the school after teaching in a grammar school, felt strongly that the best boys in the A stream were of sufficient ability to take the 'O' level G.C.E. and actively supported such a policy. Most of the other teachers of the higher streams took the view that to get the boys to take the local Leaving Certificate was enough and that to enter them for G.C.E. papers after a fifth year at school would be to mislead the pupils with hopes of academic success beyond their powers. There is also little doubt that some of these teachers were reluctant to take forms to G.C.E. level since they had never done so and were uneasy about their competence to do so. When the C.S.E. was introduced to the school, an examination which would require the pupils to stay on for a fifth year, little pressure was brought on the boys to enter for it. Although the Headmaster sent a letter to parents, no meeting was held for them at the school, and I have no evidence of active encouragement of gifted but reluctant pupils to stay on,[3] even though a few parents came to discuss the future of their sons with the Headmaster.

The school, when compared with a grammar school, cannot be expected to exhibit many of the 'academic' trappings which are traditionally associated with grammar schools. The school, despite its newness, lacked many basic facilities such as adjacent playing-fields; there was no sixth-form; only a quarter of the staff were University graduates; the curriculum was not geared to the General Certificate of Education. But the non-academic atmosphere of Lumley expressed itself in more fundamental ways. The pupils possessed no school property; they were not issued with pens, pencils, rulers, rubbers, text-books and exercise-books for which they were held responsible. As the boys moved from room to room with every change of subject on the curriculum, such basic equipment was distributed and collected at the beginning and end of each lesson. This was, of course, remarkably time-consuming, and it was not by any means exceptional for fifteen of the thirty-five minutes of the lesson to be spent in this way. The problem of time consumed in non-academic matters became even more acute during the second period of the day, since the last ten minutes of the lesson were allocated to the distribution of milk. In a few cases, the teacher insisted that he personally would undertake the issue of all equipment. One teacher, of A and B streams, aware of this not inconsiderable time loss, had the pupils pick up a pencil out of the rack on entering the room, and left the exercise and text books in the desks. This meant that the lesson could commence with a minimum of delay, but this teacher was exceptional. The rest distributed equipment every lesson, allowed the boys to choose their own seats, and seemed comparatively unconcerned about the expenditure of so much teaching time.

Lessons and examinations were, as we have seen, treated with contempt by most of the boys. Copying was highly prevalent, and the use of 'cribs' in tests was a common practice. Few teachers used the method of surprise tests, which partly eliminated preparation of cribs, or devised methods of restricting cheating. Some of the end-of-term examinations which I witnessed were inadequately supervised, especially in the low streams, and the widespread use of cribs and other aids made the examination a test of ingenuity and daring rather than of individual knowledge or ability.

This lack of pressure exerted by most teachers towards academic achievement and their failure to take precautions during examinations, which partly resulted from their belief that the boys' potentialities were extremely limited, contributed to the non-academic, custodial atmosphere of the school. For many of the teachers and most of the pupils, life at school was a necessary evil. Life was directed towards a reduction of potential conflict by a minimal imposition of demands upon one another. If the upper streams passed their examinations and the lower streams did not riot, the school was, for most teachers, succeeding.

But we must move from the general to the particular. From earlier discussion we know that the higher the stream, the more favourable the attitudes to school tend to be. With reference to the teachers, as we saw in some of the Orientation Test items, the higher the stream, the greater the pupil preference for teachers who make the boys work, who keep the class under control, who punish 'messers'. This supplies some information in which we may establish the stream differences in definition of the teacher's role by pupils, and the conflict between teacher expectations and the differences in definition of the pupil role. We may add to this information by an examination of some relevant items from the Sentence Completion Test.

The first item was 'Teachers are . . .', the results to which are given in Table XX.

TABLE XX

Teachers are . . .

Form	% Positive	% Neutral	% Negative	% Not classified	N
4A	50	40	7	3	30
4B	25	46	25	4	28
4C	38	42	17	4	24
4D	5	45	45	5	22
All	31	44	22	4	104

Chi-square = 18·09   D.f. = 6   P<·01

Examples of the positive attitudes to teachers are:

. . . sensible and trustworthy.

. . . helpful when we want to know something.

. . . very polite and ready to listen and are always willing to help you out with something worrying or puzzling.

. . . helpful at times.

. . . people who have a hard time teaching children.

. . . not bad. They have their wives to keep.

Presumably the boy who wrote '. . . very peasant' accidentally omitted the letter 'l'. The neutral category consisted of answers which contained both positive and negative elements.

. . . sometimes alright and then they are people you would like to kick when down.

. . alright at times, but they go mad if you do anything wrong

. . . alright but they tend to ignore some pupils.

. . . good except for the odd few that are stupid.

. . . smashing in some ways and lowsy in others.

. . . in between half good and half terrible.

Amongst the negative category were included:

. . . too strict.

. . . boring.

. . . a load of bums.

. . . people who expect too much from boys.

. . . a load of bull especially when they start talking about long hair and getting a job.

. . . daft and they expect you to work all day without rest.

. . . bent, mad, eccentric, crackers.

. . . horrible.

The tendency for the higher stream boys to be more favourable towards teachers is very marked; 50 per cent of 4A but 5 per cent of 4D give favourable responses; 45 per cent of 4D but 7 per cent of 4A give unfavourable responses.

The boys in lower streams not only regard the teachers less favourably, but also perceive their relationships with teachers as much less adequate. This is revealed in the answers to the item, 'Teachers here think of me as . . .'. Table XXI shows the distribution of answers.

Amongst the positive replies were:

. . . easy to get on with.

. . . a not bad sportsman, and works hard, dependable, truthful.

. . . well behaved, sensible, reliable.

. . . an intelligent good mannered boy who tries to learn what he's taught.

. . . a boy you can get on with.

. . . good mannered and helpful.

. . . somebody who when he is told to work, he works.

TABLE XXI

Teachers here think of me as . . .

Form	% Positive	% Neutral	% Negative	% Not classified	N
4A	43	23	10	23	30
4B	54	25	11	11	28
4C	33	21	17	29	24
4D	5	14	73	9	22
All	26	21	26	18	104

Chi-square = 31·99   D.f. = 6   P<·001

. . . very quiet and a good worker.

. . . hardworking (most of the time) well mannered (I hope) and I try to look smart.

Examples of the neutral category are:

. . . not bad some days, but rotten other days.

. . . an idiot at times but alright at others.

. . . normal.

. . . some think I am soft and a snob, some think I am well mannered and pleasant.

. . . average.

. . . an ordinary boy.

. . . sometimes helpful and sometimes hopless.

. . . an idiot at times but alright at others.

The negative responses included:

. . . a villain who would rather play about than do work, which is true.

. . . a timewaster.

. . . a bad boy.

. . . hopeless.

. . . a trouble maker and a cheeky one at that.

. . . a big bully and a great big long haired nit.

. . . a boy who keeps playing truant.

. . . a dodger in work.

. . . a person who is not right because I have long hair.

One again these responses are highly stream related: 73 per cent of the D stream give negative replies, whereas only 10 per cent of the A stream do so.

In short, the higher the stream, the more favourably the pupils regard the teachers, and the more positively they assess their relationship with the teachers. This, of course, is consonant with the normative structure of the streams. In the A stream, the pupils are positively orientated towards the teachers' values, and so will like the teachers and have good relationships with them. In the lower streams, the pupils are orientated against the teachers' values and dislike the teachers, who, they perceive, regard them as villains and trouble-makers. This difference leads to varied reactions to the teaching situation. Table XXII gives the results to the categorization of responses to the item 'When the teacher tell me my work is bad, I . . .'

TABLE XXII

When the teacher tells me my work is bad, I . . .

Form	% Positive	% Negative	% Not classified	N
4A	87	7	7	30
4B	65	29	7	28
4C	67	21	12	24
4D	36	27	36	22
All	65	20	14	104

Chi-square $= 7.82$ D.f. $= 3$ $P < .05$

where 87 per cent of 4A and 36 per cent of 4D give positive responses, such as

... I try and make it better.

... I try and put my standard up.

... I think to myself, I must do better than this.

... I feel ashamed and try to better it.

... I work harder.

but 7 per cent of 4A and 27 per cent of 4D give negative responses, such as

... I feel I could belt him.

... I don't listen to him. To me it is Okay.

... I don't really care.

... I just give him a dirty look.

... I always call him behind my breath.

... I go on strike.

The same trends appear in response to the item 'When lessons are boring, I . . .' as Table XXIII demonstrates.

TABLE XXIII

When lessons are boring, I . . .

Form	% Positive	% Neutral	% Negative	% Not classified	N
4A	27	57	13	3	30
4B	7	50	36	7	28
4C	4	42	42	13	24
4D	0	45	45	9	22
All	11	49	33	8	104

When the positive and neutral categories are combined
Chi-square $= 9.62$ D.f. $= 3$ $P < .05$

The replies are divided into three categories. The positive includes those which indicate that an active attempt to make use of the lesson is made.

... I try to take an interest in the work.

... I try to interest myself in the subject as much as I can.

... I try to make the best possible use of the time.

... I listen more intensely to really find out what they are talking about.

The neutral or passive category includes those responses where the pupil neither makes active use of nor tries to undermine the lesson.

... I daydream.

... I think of my night life.

... I just sit and stare out of the window until the bell goes.

... I just sit there.

... I sit and suffer because it only causes trouble if you don't.

The negative category comprises those responses which would entail a definite disturbance to the lesson.

... I start talking.

... I throw pens and a battle starts.

... I start to shout.

... I start talking and messing about and throwing ink about.

... I stop my work and have a chat.

... I go to the toilet for a smoke.

Here again the questionnaire results support our observations of the normative structure of the different streams.

The positive orientation of 4A boys to academic achievement sometimes led to criticism of those teachers who failed to elicit the requisite standards of work.

I don't like Mr. ——— 'cos he can't teach properly. You don't learn anything. He's just talk, talk, talk.

I think the Head should stop Mr. ——— teaching here. He really is a bit of a nutter.

I'm sure Mr. ——— can't control us, but I suppose it isn't his fault.

Mr. ——— is just an extra and I don't think he should be on the staff.

I don't like Science 'cos I don't know what Mr. ——— is talking about half the time.

Mr. ——— is the best of all teachers 'cos he makes maths so simple and easy.

Such intolerance of teacher incompetence was almost entirely confined to the A stream, since such failure inhibited their academic attainment. In the low streams incompetent or eccentric teachers formed a good basis for 'having fun' or 'messing'.

Why is it that by the fourth year at Lumley School the pupils' attitudes to the teachers and their conception of the teacher-pupil relationship have diverged so fundamentally? To indicate, as we have done, that such attitudes are consistent with the normative structure of different forms tells us little about *the process* by which both of these develop. A definite answer cannot be attempted here; it must suffice if we indicate some of the ways in which the teachers influence the process.

One element we must consider is the bias of the teachers towards members of the A streams, for these boys were, in the first place, most likely to take examinations successfully in the fourth year: they were the academic elite, the boys who were in ability, achievement and values closest to the teachers. The staff were thus anxious to create an academic atmosphere in the form.

The form teacher of the first year A stream felt a need to establish as early as possible an awareness amongst these pupils of being an A stream, and regretted that the boys seemed to resist these pressures for the first two years in school.

I've tried several times to make them feel like an A stream, but it's not much use at this stage.

Invidious comparisons were frequently made by teachers between the different streams. Most frequently this occurred when an A class misbehaved. On one form blackboard I found the notice:

We must always remember to behave as an A class.

On one occasion a teacher left the room to investigate some noise in the corridor. 'Who are you lot?' he cried. '3B, sir,' came the reply. 'You sound more like 1E than 3B!' was the master's crushing retort. The point is that he did not compare their behaviour with that of a first form, but with the E stream of the first year. On another occasion a teacher took a number of boys to visit the local Courts. As his numbers had to be limited, he selected the prefects out of 4A and made up the party with those who had the highest positions in the history examination. The rest were placed in the charge of another teacher, who decided that they would clean up his room. At this news the boys groaned and protested. The teacher softened the blow by saying:

> You're the only form in the school that I can trust. I wouldn't dare let 4E do a job like this. They'd make a complete mess of it. You ought to be complimented.

The favourite saying of another teacher was:

> We like to think the A stream have more common sense than the rest. Do you want to let us down?

One teacher, when members of 4B were misbehaving, said:

> This is 4B. You wouldn't believe that this was next to the top class. Does B stand for blockheads?

Some teachers felt that not only were the A stream to be made conscious of their superiority, but that they should also maintain a certain social distance from other forms. One teacher, for example, told me that if he saw a member of the A stream going with a boy from the lower stream, he would discourage the friendship.

> I tell him to go round with the lads in his own form. 'They're not for you,' I tell him.

The tendency towards favouritism of the A stream becomes evident in more concrete ways. The selection of prefects, for example, shows a very heavy bias, since it is predominantly A and B stream pupils who are considered most suitable for appointment by the Headmaster and staff. During the academic year 1964-5, fifteen of the prefects came from 4A, seven from 4B, two from 4C and three from 4D. Thus half the 4A boys were elected prefects and gained considerable status in their own and younger boys' eyes. Further, since prefects' duties are a delegation of staff authority, appointment led to an intensification of their sense of unity with the teachers.

When the school organized holidays, the number of applications frequently exceeded the number of available places. Once again the bias towards high stream boys appears. In order to reduce the length of the list, the teacher in charge would consult other members of staff about the applicants. Boys who received unfavourable reports were deleted from the list and would be told at a later stage that they had been 'unlucky in the draw'. Another way in which 'undesirables' could be excluded from the holiday was to publicize the projected journey primarily to A and B stream boys, who would be actively encouraged to join the school party. The teachers justified themselves on the grounds that the difficult low stream boys were a potential threat to the success of the holiday, and that in any case they could not reasonably be expected to give up their own holidays merely to exhaust themselves in exerting strict control over uncooperative and recalcitrant pupils. Although there is little doubt that the majority of the applicants were from A and B streams, this selection process reduced the actual proportion of C and D stream boys admitted to these holidays. Of the pupils taken on various holidays between 1961 and 1965, 66 per cent came from the A and B streams.

Most important of all, the organization of the school time-table reflected this concern with the higher streams at the expense of the lower ones. Table XXIV gives the allocation of teachers to the boys in the fourth year.

Mr. A and Mr. B taught 4A and 4B for nearly half the school week. Mr. A was the Deputy Headmaster. Mr. B was a graduate who left the school at the end of 1965 to become the Head teacher of another school. Both were noted as two of the most strict disciplinarians of the school. Mr. C, who taught 4C and 4D for sixteen periods each, was by no means a strict disciplinarian; most would judge him to be the reverse.

This was no accidental process. It seems to have been part of the school policy to put younger, less experienced teachers with junior forms, and although the teachers of senior forms were older and more experienced, the men with lower qualifications

TABLE XXIV

Teacher Allocation

Subject	4A Teacher	4B Teacher	4C Teacher	4D Teacher	Periods
Maths	A	A	C	C	8
English	B	B	C	C	8
Science	D	D	D	D	3
Art	E/F	E/F	E/F	E/F	4
Geography	G	G	G	G	2
Music	H	H	H	H	2
T.D.	J	J	J	J	2
R.E.	K	K	K	K	2
Handicraft	L/M/N	L/M/N	L/M/N	L/M/N	4
P.E.	O	O	O	O	1
History	B	P	P	P	2

and/or weaker discipline were given the lower streams.[4] (This is not to say that teachers with lower qualifications are poorer teachers.) The resulting variation in experience of the teaching situation for boys in different streams cannot be ignored, for although all the fourth year boys shared the same teachers for half of their periods, the C and D stream boys in the third and fourth years tended to be taught by teachers with lower qualifications, lower status in terms of allowances and weaker discipline than in the case of A and B stream boys. This allocation could be justified by the Headmaster on the grounds that the A and B stream boys take external examinations and must therefore be taught by the better teachers.

Since all teachers are 'tested out' by pupils to see 'how far they can go', pupils with less strict teachers will build up different concepts of acceptable behaviour to boys with more strict teachers. The policy of placing lower streams under the supervision of less competent and less strict teachers has the effect of giving these pupils extended expectations about the kind of behaviour which will be tolerated from them, and thus of granting the high status pupils even greater control over the deviant behaviour which in any case becomes normative in lower streams by the fourth year. The school's method of allocating teachers may thus reinforce those processes by which lower stream pupils deviate increasingly from the school's expectations as they progress through their four years at Lumley.

The significance of the allocation of teachers becomes more clear when we examine the background to 4A and 4D in the *third* year. The form teacher of 3A (now the 4A in this study) was extremely proud of his class. In his opinion they were the best form he had ever had. Under his guidance, they developed a strong esprit de corps. He admitted to me that on occasions he may have exceeded normal bounds in fostering this in-group loyalty, but he felt that basically the achievement of some sense of unity was beneficial to the boys and to the school. This in-group loyalty was further increased by the sense of rivalry between 3B and 3A over such matters as football, house-points, contributions to the school fund, the Attendance Shield and so on.[5] In the words of the 3A teacher,

They couldn't bear not being on top in everything.

During the year of the study, this teacher became very nostalgic about his old form. Several times during the year he compared his present 3A very unfavourably with their predecessors. On one occasion, when a member of his present 3A was standing outside the Headmaster's study for being late, he said:

Last year it was completely unknown for a boy in 3A to be standing against that wall. It just shows you the different standards. I'm disgusted.

On another occasion he mused sadly about the record his old 3A had achieved – winning the Attendance shield for nine consecutive weeks.

It is, of course, impossible to measure the extent of this or any other teacher's influence on the normative structure of 4A; but it is important to consider this influence. The third year background of the present 4D sharpens our understanding of the importance of the teacher.

Whereas 3A were moulded into a form with strong group loyalties and an internalized wish to excel, 3D seems to have been subjected to depressing and inhibiting forces. In the words of their form teacher, who took them for nearly half the lessons,

You just can't afford to trust that lot.

In practice he carried out this policy to the letter. In order to reduce theft – which did occur with less strict teachers – all the equipment was kept locked in the cupboard. The teacher distributed all the equipment himself and then locked the cupboard. If a boy required a new pencil or rubber, the teacher would go through the process of locking and unlocking the cupboard. Occasionally the boys would ask needlessly for materials simply to watch the master performing this extensive ritual. The boys were thus given no responsibility – he even sharpened their pencils himself.

The policy of this teacher in Mathematics was based on the correct assumption that most of the pupils in 3D were far from expert at the theory or practice of simple mathematical calculations, and had not fully memorized the multiplication tables. His method was thus to take each pupil back to the most basic mathematical computations and allow him to progress from that point. This meant that few of the pupils were doing the same work at the same time, whereas in 3A the slow boys were forced to keep up with the rate the teacher imposed. Most of the boys worked from text books which give endless lists of repetitive exercises. Any mistake was penalized by repetition of the page of work. Thus, one slight error would lead to a considerable delay in the boy's progress. It is hardly surprising that most of the boys failed to make progress, became bored and tried to undermine the lessons.

If you didn't like working with Mr. —— all you had to do when he was giving the books out was to, 'Tut, tut, tut,' and he'd go, 'Right, that's it!' and collect all the books in and you'd have to sit there while he talked to you. And then about five minutes before the end of the lesson he'd give the books out and you'd just put the title and the bell would go.

Mr. ⸺ wasn't like other teachers. He used to just let us sit there without doing our work. He wouldn't give you any work unless you were quiet. He used to give [two low status boys] all the privileges, you know what I mean? If he had an errand he used to send them. He used to give them books as well. He gives them books to take home with them for a test and we didn't get none so they used to come top.

I don't like the work here. In the first year we was doing addition and all that and we're still doing that now. We can do it, but we're still doing it. It's not worth it, is it? if you're doing nowt. When we was in third year we had Mr. ⸺ for the first time. We started again from first year with all these simple add-ups and that. Addition, it's easy that. But if you did owt wrong you had to do it all again. We'd have done harder work better.

We should have learnt more in third year, but we didn't. We learnt nowt off Mr. ⸺.

Of course, the boys in these lower streams were much more difficult for teachers than boys in higher streams, especially by the third or fourth years. Discipline becomes an important problem and most of the boys make a show of not being interested in the lessons. Attempts to sabotage the lesson would result in lessons where the teacher was not firmly in control and prepared to take firm action. But the point here is that the teachers unknowingly contribute to this process by their rejection of these lower stream boys as 'unintelligent louts'. Dave (99), who held the top position on the informal status ranking in 4D, was described by this teacher in his report to the Headmaster at the end of third year as:

Mediocre; untidy in every way; lazy; doesn't care two pins for anyone except himself; vicious; sly; smoker; uncooperative; liar; paranoiac; moaner; bully; hates anyone intelligent; trouble-maker.

A less favourable report is hardly possible. Yet much of it was true. Whenever possible, he would shout wildly and distract or provoke other boys. Most of his time at school was spent in a search for distractions. He would laugh openly if a teacher told him that his school work would help him to get a good job. Most of his actions were directed to 'getting a laugh' and he would revel in the guffaws that emanated from the rest of the class when a prank was successful or a teacher fell into his trap. When rebuked or punished he would sulk if he could not lie himself out of the situation.

Yet this behaviour represents an adaptation to a situation. In part it is a necessary adjustment to a situation in which he is a member of a stream whose members are penalized in favour of upper and especially A streams. He has learned to be seen as a relative failure. His relationships with teachers deteriorated steadily over the four years until he was totally rejected by many. He made virtually no progress at his work. In short, the allocation of teachers, the tendency for teachers to favour higher stream boys, and the kind of relationships teachers made with the boys contribute in a fundamental way to the values of the boys. Whilst the A stream boys progress in all the ways which the teacher regards as important, and thus create a teaching situation which is rewarding to both, the D stream boys become increasingly slow and difficult and create a situation which becomes mutually dissatisfying.

The boys were, of course, not unaware of the privileges conferred on high stream boys by the teachers.

I think we've got more privileges than 4C and 4D have. There's more prefects picked from our class and from 4A than from them. They've been treated different to us, you know, we've been treated kindly and they've been treated rough. It's perhaps only slightly, but it makes a big difference. You know, the teachers pick on them 'cos they've got long hair and dirty shoes and dirty clothes. They don't see why they're picked on. If they was to watch themselves doing things they'd know they was doing wrong.

(B stream boy)

I just don't like [4A and 4B] getting treated better than us, you know what I mean? They call them by their first name and everything. They just treat us as though we're not there. One or two call me by my first name, but not many. But I'm not really bothered about that. I've got that all through school.

(D stream boy)

I'd drop dead if they called me [by my first name].

They're [teachers] not interested in use. It's all 4A and 4B. 'Cos they never take us out [on school visits] do they? I admit there's a few that's scruffy in our class and you can't take them all out but if they just picked the ones that aren't so scruffy it would be different.

(D stream boy)

It's dead cushy at this school. You don't do owt. You're supposed to do writing but they don't check the books so you don't have to do it.

(D stream boy)

I don't think they bother about us here. They can't do 'cos they don't mark our books. If [the Headmaster] saw our books he'd go mad 'cos of all the things wrote over them. Mr. ——— doesn't say owt.

(D stream boy)

[The Head] calls you, don't he? He calls you rotten and gives you a lecture. He tells you you're a layabout and all that and tells you to get your hair cut. And if you don't you won't get a reference. But I don't want a reference.

(Clint)

This chapter has been primarily concerned with the ways in which the allocation and attitudes of teachers are related to the differentiation between streams of the pupils' attitudes to teachers. Whilst it is true that boys in different streams are faced with different problems of adaptation to the teaching situation, it is also important to consider the variety of modes of adaptation of the teachers themselves. We are not so much concerned with how *new* teachers adapt to their careers, but with how the *experienced* teachers who taught the third and fourth year pupils adapted to the forms they taught daily. The Headmaster at Lumley allocated the more competent teachers to the higher streams and the less competent ones to the lower streams. The argument here is that this system of allocation reinforces the teacher's basic mode of adaptation and the sense of his own competence. When a teacher is allocated to mainly high stream pupils, this is perceived as a reward to his competence to teach, and because it is easier to teach the higher streams, where the children are more motivated to work hard and not misbehave, the competence will increase. When a teacher is allocated to low streams, this is perceived as a recognition of his limitations as a teacher, and the lack of interest in academic work and tendencies towards misbehaviour evinced by lower stream pupils reinforce the teacher's sense of his own incompetence.

Teachers have a number of basic problems. The class must be under the firm control of the teacher; the children must learn; the children must show evidence of their learning. The more competent teachers who tend to be assigned to higher streams can solve these problems with comparative ease. The children are not difficult to control. The previous history of A or B stream children has prepared them to behave well in class, to regard themselves as the academic and behavioural elite, to be interested in academic achievement. The teacher thus has little difficulty in persuading the children to work hard and to give evidence of their learning in external examinations in the fourth year. The existence of these examinations encourages the teacher to teach the children and the results confirm his competence to teach.

For teachers of low streams, it is much more difficult to control the class; discipline becomes a much more important problem than in high streams. The pupils are much less motivated to work and thus seek to undermine the efforts exerted by the teacher towards academic achievement. Since these low stream boys do not take external examinations, the ways in which evidence of either the pupils' academic achievement or the teacher's competence can be assessed are restricted. The less competent teachers who tend to be assigned to low streams are faced with much more difficult problems than their colleagues with high streams. At Lumley, low stream teachers adapt to their situation in two basic ways. The first mode of adaptation is that of *withdrawal*. Because this type of teacher is less competent in matters of discipline yet is assigned to forms with the greatest discipline problems, he avoids the problem by ignoring its existence. He does this by sitting in his desk at the front, marking boys' work or some similar activity, whilst the rest of the class continue to enjoy the relative chaos which reigns. The class members are frequently at different stages in each subject so that no check can be made on individual or group progress. Alternatively, withdrawal can take the form of lecturing to the class in a voice sufficiently loud to drown the voices of misbehaving pupils. In this way the teacher appears to be teaching, even though the pupils complete little work. The second mode of adaptation for the less competent teachers with low streams is that of *domination*. This type of teacher imposes a completely rigid discipline, infringements of which incur severe penalties. Because silence reigns in the form, the children appear to be working hard. In reality, they make little effort; they become increasingly bored by the lesson, their interest in the subject declines, and they seek to undermine the authority of the teacher by disturbing the lesson without being apprehended.

In short, the allocation of teachers to upper or lower streams on the basis of teacher competence reinforces the dominant trends of the peer group; the pupils in higher forms increase in achievement and improve their relationships with teachers whom they like, and the pupils in lower streams become increasingly retarded and their relationships with teachers deteriorate to the point of mutual toleration at best and mutual hostility at worst.[6]

Teachers do not approach their pupils without preconceptions; they possess a set of values or expectations concerning the ways in which pupils *ought* to behave. These role expectations concerning the pupil have been detailed in earlier chapters and require no repetition here. We need only remember that 'good' pupils, those who conform to the expectations, come from higher streams, and that 'bad' pupils, those who deviate from the expectations, come from lower streams.

Whenever two people meet they are forced to make assessments of each other, by taking each other's behaviour, whether verbalized or gestured, into account.[7] The first impressions determine to some degree the form and extent of further interaction. The teacher-pupil relationship in any single case will be a function of many factors, not least of which are the personality and the past experience of the individuals concerned, but every such interaction will have certain common structural similarities. In a secondary school, where teachers usually take large classes for just one or two subjects, the actual interaction between a teacher and any one pupil will be relatively brief. Indeed, it often happens that a teacher does not directly speak to any one pupil for several consecutive lessons. The teacher thus tends to make *indirect* assessments of the pupil, and these will be largely determined by the child's conformity to the teacher's role expectations.[8] For example, the standard of work produced by a pupil will be taken as a basic guide to a more general assessment.

When a teacher takes a new class, he will tend to divide the class into three categories. Firstly, the 'good' pupils who conform to his expectations. Secondly, the 'bad' pupils who deviate. Thirdly, those who are not outstanding in either conformity or deviation. It is the names of the pupils in the first two categories that are learned immediately by the teacher. For those in the residual category, actual names are learned very much more slowly, so that a teacher often has difficulty in connecting the name and the face.

These inferences which the teacher draws in such a highly selective way from the pupils' behaviour, and the 'categorization process' to which it leads, act as a definition of the situation in which teachers and pupils find themselves. This definition provides the plan for all future interaction between the two parties. Because the inferences are selected from limited aspects of the child's behaviour and are interpreted in terms of the teacher's role expectations, there is a constant danger of mis-interpretation. The teacher may draw conclusions which are unjustified when we consider the totality of the child's behaviour.

In a streamed school the teacher categorizes the pupils not only in terms of the inferences he makes from the child's classroom behaviour but also from the child's stream level. It is for this reason that the teacher can rebuke an A stream boy for behaving like a D stream boy. The teacher has learned to *expect* certain kinds of behaviour from members of different streams.

In short, the teacher tends to categorize pupils on the basis of stream and the inferences he makes from the child's behaviour and the extent to which it conforms to his role expectations of the pupil. This, of course, is a process of interaction which is entirely 'natural'; it is part of the everyday life of us all. Although the process of categorization may have a real basis, it may also have effects which are deleterious to the self-conception and development of the pupil, and it is these latent effects which we must elucidate. An example of the influence of stream, as we have seen, is that the A stream pupils develop a sense of superiority over the others, who, aware of their implied inferiority, come to regard the A stream boys as 'snobs'.

There are, within the teacher's situation, certain factors which tend to exacerbate this process of categorization. One such factor is the informal gossip among the staff. Whenever teachers discuss pupils, they import into the discussion their own interpretations and preconceptions, which provide the 'naïve' teacher, that is one who has no direct contact with the child, with information which categorizes the child in advance of actual interaction and defines the situation in terms of the behaviour the teacher should expect. I do not wish to suggest that teachers always take their colleagues' opinions about pupils as an established fact; to do so would be to distort the situation seriously. On numerous occasions teachers disagree about the behaviour of a pupil with comments such as 'He's not like that in my lesson.' But disagreement can only occur between teachers who both have direct experience of the child. To the *naïve* teacher, opinions of colleagues will have the effect of acting as a provisional agent of the categorization process. In other words, one of the functions of teachers' gossip about pupils is to add to the preconceptions and expectations by which a pupil is assessed. This may be particularly true for new teachers, or for those who request information about a class prior to taking them for the first time. The form teacher of 3C at Lumley told me how he expected that Clint would be a very difficult boy on the basis of comments from his colleagues, and was very surprised to find that he 'had no trouble with him'.

Perhaps the most important and only partially recognized effect of categorization is the way in which this process sets up counter-expectations in the pupil. Because a teacher has categorized a pupil, however provisionally, he may in his own behaviour toward the pupil emit expectations to which the relatively immature pupil will conform. This bi-product of categorization will be most marked at the extremes, that is, with the 'good' and 'bad' pupils. It would hardly be surprising if 'good' pupils thus become 'better' and the 'bad' pupils become 'worse'. It is, in short, an example of a self-fulfilling prophecy.[9] The negative expectations of the teacher reinforce the negative behavioural tendencies. Let us consider some examples.

One day in the Spring Term the Youth Employment Officer

visited the school to speak to the boys in the fourth year. As he
left the Hall at the end of the speech, someone began to cheer.
The Deputy Head teacher, who was standing on the platform,
pointed down to the boys and shouted, 'You! Go to my room!'
The boy who had cheered was a prefect, but Don of 4D stood
up, even though he had not cheered. It was as if he expected
to be rebuked even when he had committed no crime.

On another occasion I was observing a lesson in Handicraft.
The boys were tidying the workshop in anticipation of the final
bell of the school day. As there were several minutes to spare,
I asked the teacher if I could send a boy across the road to buy
some stamps from the Post Office for me. The teacher agreed,
and I asked Derek, the high status boy from 4D. The teacher
turned to me and said, 'You don't want to send him if you want
to get those stamps today,' and asked another boy to run the
errand. Derek, who seemed both surprised and pleased by my
request now began to scowl. When I insisted that Derek should
go for me, Derek looked at me and said, 'Are you sure?' He felt
that it would be more appropriate if I agreed with the teacher's
conception of him.

During one Art lesson the teacher picked up a painting done
by Derek and took it to the front of the class. When he called
the form to attention and said, 'Boys, look what Derek's done,'
Derek immediately began to laugh delightedly. But when the
teacher continued, 'This is a very good picture', Derek was
overwhelmed with confusion and embarrassment. He had assumed that the teacher was using his picture as an illustration of
bad work.

It is important to stress that if this effect of categorization is
real, it is entirely unintended by the teachers. They do not wish
to make low streams more difficult than they are! But it does
imply that the teacher needs consciously to adapt away from these
effects if he does not wish to reinforce the negative self-concep-
tions of lower stream boys. To treat 'bad' pupils as 'good'
pupils may appear to be unrealistic, but it may be a form of
manipulation which is essential to the teacher if he is to change
the values and attitudes of those pupils who turn against the
system of the school.

Chapter Six

THE DELINQUENT GROUP

Boys who commit crimes do not admit them easily, least of all to the teachers who represent authority and the midle-class values of honesty. Yet the reader will have deduced from our discussion that Lumley Secondary Modern School contained a number of boys who were delinquent in the sense that they had committed offences which had resulted in an appearance in the Juvenile Court. The present researcher was, of course, able to specify the extent of delinquent behaviour at Lumley through confidential consultations with the local Chief Probation Officer. Yet such information provides us merely with the *official* figures on the extent of delinquent behaviour, that is, the number of times a particular boy has been apprehended and prosecuted. It tells us nothing about the commission of offences which are 'successful', remaining undetected by the forces of law.

During my stay at Lumley I managed to discuss problems of delinquency with every boy in the fourth year. Usually I was able to approach the subject during private conversation on the basis of more general discussions, such as the behaviour of the police in the area. When I had been in the school for nearly six months, the boys began to realize that in many respects I was not like a teacher, and that matters they mentioned to me would not be reported back to the staff. By the Spring Term, therefore, most of the boys felt able to trust me with their various confidences and, with two exceptions, seemed happy to discuss the extent of their own and others' delinquency. From what the boys reported I was able to take two measures. The first was the number of times every boy in the fourth year had appeared in the Juvenile Court, figures which could be confirmed from the official records. In this respect I found no example of a boy who denied an appearance in Court but was subsequently proved a liar by the records. The second measure was the unverifiable admission by each boy whether or not he was engaged in petty thieving and shoplifting.

The results of these two measures are given in Table XXV.

TABLE XXV

Delinquency

Form	% Who Admit at Least One Appearance in Court	% Who Admit Current Petty Thieving	N
4A	3	7	30
4B	14	43	28
4C	37	73	22
4D	55	64	22
All	24	43	102

These figures conform to the trends we have noted previously: negative behaviour is associated with lowness of stream. In the D stream over half the boys have appeared at least once in Court *and* admit current petty larceny. By contrast, in 4A only one boy has a Court conviction, and that was some years previously, and only two boys admit current thieving. It could be argued, of course, that the low proportion of boys in 4A who admit delinquent activities does not represent the true figures at all, but is merely a measure of the extent to which such boys feel shame and thus reluctance to admit their offences to one who in school seemed dangerously allied to the teachers in whose eyes they were anxious to secure high esteem. Whether or not this is so remains unanswerable. That this factor is an important one in our interpretation of Table XXV does not seem to be very likely, since it does not agree with the free and honest discussion they were able to hold with the researcher. Should this factor be important, the figures are still of significance since they are an index of the differential willingness of boys to be candid about their crimes.

From the figures it is clear that delinquency plays an important part in the normative structure of 4A in so far as its absence is indicative of norms *against* breaking the law. There seems little doubt from the discussion with these A boys that home environment was a force in establishing within these boys values which exclude criminal tendencies. The brief data on home background to be given in Chapter Seven gives some support to this contention. For the moment, suffice it to say that most of these non-delinquent boys, especially those in 4A, regarded the possibility of future delinquency with complete horror. Even Alf, the only 4A boy to have appeared in Court, reported his parents' reaction as follows:

I'm still black and blue. I wouldn't like to do it again. Oh, no. I didn't really understand.

Other parental reactions, or rather potential reactions as imagined by the boys, were similarly reported.

You don't know how strict my father is!

My brother's been in [court], but you won't catch me there.

Why should I nick anything? If I want something I can ask my Mam and Dad for the money.

I'd be too afraid to nick owt. You've too much to lose.

It's not worth it. You can find better things to do, can't you?

I wouldn't nick from round here, they might tell my Mam.

I wouldn't. I've got good parents.

I've been tempted, but I never would.

It's not worth it, is it? For something worth a few shillings You get a record then, don't you?

I've never had to nick anything. I've always had some like money in my pocket.

If anyone asked me to start nicking I'd put my coat on and go home. I'd really get it off my Mam if I got into trouble with the police. I know that. I've enough sense not to do it.

Although part of the explanation for the lack of delinquency in the A stream derives from the home background, this is not in itself a sufficient explanation. Were it as simple as this, then we should not find any delinquent boy in the school with parents with anti-criminal values. In reality, as we shall see, some of the boys who were highly involved in petty theft knew only too well that apprehension would completely appal their parents. Many other factors, such as the personality of the individual, must be involved. The factor we wish to stress here is the pressure in the peer group. The norms in 4A would *necessarily* have to proscribe delinquent behaviour, since this would be inconsistent with the other predominating norms, which advocated behaviour in conformity with the teachers' expectations. To accept and internalize the teachers' values is to reject delinquent behaviour. 'Good lads do not steal.' Such support for these values as comes from the home will act in two ways. It will *predispose* boys to accepting the teachers' role expectations and to being integrated into the A stream, and it will *reinforce* the group's own norms. Likewise, where neither the group nor the home prohibit delinquent behaviour, the forces will draw the boy towards delinquency. In those cases where the home influence is not sharply defined in this respect, the peer group norms will become increasingly powerful in determining the attitude and values and behaviour of the boy.

The boys in 4B represent once again a compromise between the A and the C/D streams. Although only 14 per cent have appeared in Court, 43 per cent admit current petty larceny, which is a sharp increase on the 7 per cent in the A stream. Not surprisingly this figure disproportionately represents those boys of *high* informal status in the form: 9 of the 12 boys admitting petty larceny come from the upper half of the form and includes the first five positions of the informal status hierarchy. Take Basher as an example:

> I've been to Court three times. Throwing a stone on a man's head. Smashing thirty windows, but I said I'd only done two. And breaking in . . . with seven others.

He described this last event as follows:

> We just went in. The door was open. We went up the stairs

and this door was open with all things in, so we just started getting them. There was a guitar and about six trumpets and a lot of other things. When we came down this door was locked so we kicked it and smashed the glass and about three days later — got caught in town. And he told on the rest.

More frequent in 4B is simple shoplifting. Basher continues:

We did summat about two weeks ago, in Woolies. About six records. ———— was there and he passed them to me and I hid them under my coat. ———— was keeping in front of the woman so she couldn't see us . . . There's not much risk in getting caught. Last week we got two ties out of the ———— shop. We just walked in and said, 'Have you got any jeans?' and while he went to get them we got two ties, me and ———— . . . We was coming home from Rugby on Saturday and we went in a shop and got five barm cakes and just walked out. And just as we was walking out, this bloke came into the shop and said, 'What do you want?' so I asked him for the time.

Less typically, Basher was willing to steal on his own as well as in the group.

I used to work in a cafe. I was coming out one night and I left the window open. There was these cigarettes on a shelf near the window and I left it loose. I went back about twelve o'clock and got about eighty cigs. and the next night I got about a hundred. They never found out and I kept working there.

Bert was as highly involved in this behaviour as Basher. His reputation amongst the boys for skill and daring was considerable.

Bert's the worst. We went in this shop – we had a penny – and we asked for a half-penny chew and went round the counter and got two minerals. And then Bert went in again and asked for another half-penny chew and got another. That's Bert, that was.

The boys took risks, but they relied on the fact that many shops will not easily prosecute.

I got caught last September. I was up town, you know, swiping books and pens and when we come out this copper and a woman got hold of us and took us in this room and said, 'Empty your pockets.' So we emptied them and he says, 'Right, if we find you up here again you'll be in court.' He just took the stuff off us and that was the end of it.

In some cases the home pressures were strong and won: as one low status boy reported:

I haven't really got the guts to swipe anything. I don't really want to. I get all I really want at home. I don't need to pinch anything. My dad's always saying, 'You don't want to pinch anything.'

But for those of higher status, for those who aspired to be among the leading members of the form, the pressures towards delinquency for the peer group were increased.

If my Mam and Dad knew I was going with a lad who'd been to court they'd try to stop me going with him. Only I'd still go with him you know.

(Informal status 16)

I've done my bit.

(Informal status 17)

This last comment was spoken with such reluctance and embarrassment that it implied that the boy felt it necessary to make his contribution in spite of feelings against theft. The group pressures can be so powerful that only exceptionally strong personalities can resist them. 46, with an informal status rank 6, was such a boy:

My Mam's told me not to [steal] since I was young. The others just take it in their stride. They nicked some barm cakes from a shop the other day. And they don't think anything of it. If they try to nick something when I'm there, I say, 'You're not coming with me if you're going to do things like that.' Alf [of 4A] used to do it, but he stopped when I was with him, 'cos every time he said he was going to do something I just went and he stopped . . . If I haven't got the money I just leave it. You know, a thing like that could get worse, you know what I mean? And as they get older and keep on doing it, but if they get caught it goes against their name. You've only got to get caught once and you get put on probation. It wouldn't upset Bert. He'd probably go on stealing, you know taking things, little things, petty things, but that can amount to bigger things. It's daft. It's not worth it.

It is clear that this boy repudiated the group pressures in favour of home influence and his own 'common sense'. But it is significant that he mainly associated with boys in Clique C, not with Cliques A and B which were the centres of the delinquents. He was liked since he was clever and was always willing to help other boys with work problems. And he did not criticize unless he himself was involved. In short, he did not deviate to any marked extent from the group's norms, with the result that his non-participation in delinquent activities did not reduce his informal status. In contrast, 55, the major deviant of the form, openly criticized the delinquents when they were discussing recent exploits, which served to illustrate his deviance and arouse rejection. As Basher reported:

> Three-quarters of the boys in this school swipe things. Nearly everyone in our class has except 55. He's too posh him. He's always saying 'No, Basher, you shouldn't swear and steal', you know, in a posh voice. You have to hit him to shut him up. He gets on your nerves.

We would expect to find an even greater cluster of delinquent boys occupying ranks of high informal status in 4C. Such is the case: only one of the eleven boys in the upper half of the informal status ranks does not admit current thieving as against six in the lower half; six of the upper half have court records against two in the lower half. There are similar results in 4D. Nine of the eleven boys in the upper half of the informal status rank admit current thieving, against five in the lower half; and of the twelve boys with court records, only three fall in the lower half. In these two forms, therefore, we see that high status is associated with a court record and current petty thieving.

A glance at Chart V will remind the reader of the considerable overlap in friendship choice between the high status members of 4C and 4D. In our discussion we shall combine these two forms and from them derive a 'delinquent group'.[1] For purposes of convenience we shall define this group not by actual delinquency, but on the basis of friendship choice and high status. In each form there is a strong association between friendship choice and

4C BOYS | 4D BOYS

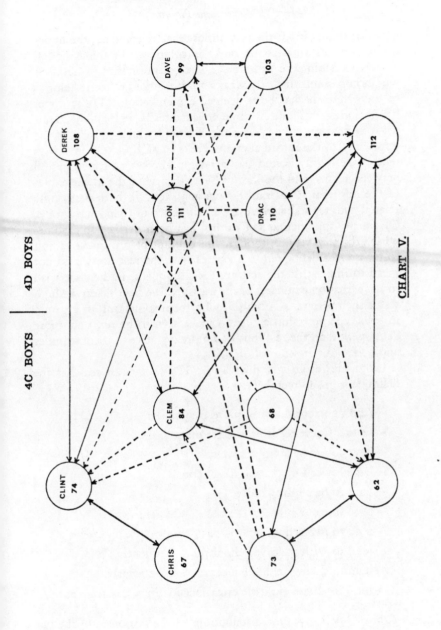

CHART V.

informal status. In 4C the two almost exactly coincide; the upper half of the informal status ranks is composed of the A and B cliques (excluding the 'aspirants'). The exception is 70 of Clique A who occupies informal status rank 14. But since he clearly belongs to the group, he has been deemed a member. In 4D the upper half includes all Clique A, three boys from Clique B and 96. Thus we have two groups: a 'delinquent group' which consists of the upper half of the informal status ranks in 4C and 4D, boys who tend to be highly bound by friendship choices both within and between forms, and the 'rest' which consists of the lower halves of the informal status ranks, boys who tend to be less strongly related within and between streams in terms of friendship choice. Of course, this 'delinquent group' has been derived in a somewhat arbitrary way. Although the delinquent group *does* admit to far greater delinquent tendencies than the rest do, we do not mean to imply that the rest are *non*-delinquent. Rather, we wish to show that on a number of the measures we have taken the high status members of 4C and 4D, who form something of a group in terms of friendship choices, can be seen to be not only more delinquent than the rest, but also more negative in their attitudes and behaviour at school.

From the results given in Table XXVI we can see that the delinquent group members:

—admit current thieving more frequently.

—have a Court record more frequently.

—have lower behaviour scores.

—have lower Orientation Test scores.

—tend to be slightly older.

—tend to smoke more.

—tend to like school less.

—tend to wish to leave school more frequently.

—tend to desire further education less frequently.

—tend to desire skilled/clerical occupations less frequently.

Table XXVII gives the distributions of the responses of the two groups to some items on the Sentence Completion Test. The delinquent group members:

TABLE XXVI

Differences between the 'Delinquent Group' and the 'Rest'

	% Admit Current Thieving	% Court Record	Behavioural Score Mean	Appearance Score Mean	Behavioural Score % above Median	Appearance Score % above Median	Orientation Test Mean Score	Orientation Test % above Median
D-GROUP	87	65	3·02	2·88	26	43	48·04	33
REST	48	24	3·81	3·43	76	57	55·10	70
ALL	68	45	3·40	3·06	50	50	51·41	52
STATISTICAL TEST	$\chi^2=6\cdot12$ D.f.$=1$ P$<\cdot025$	$\chi^2=6\cdot01$ D.f.$=1$ P$<\cdot025$	—	—	$\chi^2=13\cdot12$ D.f.$=1$ P$<\cdot001$	Not significant	—	$\chi^2=4\cdot42$ D.f.$=1$ P$<\cdot05$

	Age (Mean Years)	Mean Cigarette Consumption per Day	% Dislike School (c.f. Table V)	% Wishing to leave school (c.f. Table VI)	% Desiring further Education (c.f. Table VII)	% Desiring Class III Occupation
D-GROUP	14·91	4·44	67	84	30	43
REST	14·66	1·51	60	57	57	52
ALL	14·80	3·17	63	71	43	48

—are more negatively orientated to A stream boys.

—react less positively to boring lessons.

—react less positively to bad work.

—have more negative opinions of teachers.

TABLE XXVII

D-Group vs. Rest on the S.C. Test

Variable	Result			
Boys in 4A are . . . (cf Table XVIII)	Positive %	Neutral %	Negative %	N/C %
All	20	17	57	7
D-Gp	8	28	59	5
Rest......	35	0	55	10
When Lessons are Boring . . . (cf Table XXIII)				
All	2	43	43	11
D-Gp	0	28	64	8
Rest......	5	60	20	15
Teachers are . . . (cf Table XX)				
All	22	43	30	4
D-Gp	8	48	40	4
Rest......	35	40	20	5
Teachers Think me . . . (cf Table XXI)				
All	20	17	43	20
D-Gp	8	20	52	20
Rest......	30	15	35	20
When Teacher Tells me my Work is Bad ... (cf Table XXII)	Positive %		Negative %	N/C
All	52		24	24
D-Gp	40		32	28
Rest......	65		15	20

—perceive their relationships with teachers less positively.

In short, the delinquent group, which is defined by the high status and friendship choices of its members, contains the central core of boys whose behaviour and attitudes are negative in terms of the school's values. It is to the formation and structure of this group that we must now turn.[2]

We have already seen that the delinquent group was dominated by Clint of 4C, since this boy was the best fighter, the 'cock of the school'. He was a fairly tall but slender boy. His hair was very long, emulating the style of the Rolling Stones, the 'pop' group he most admired. According to the eleven plus examination he was one of the most intelligent boys in the school, with an I.Q. of 110. He had been a borderline case for a place in a Grammar School. On arrival at Lumley he was naturally placed in the A stream, but by the end of the first term, allegedly due to persistent misbehaviour, considerable enmity had developed between Clint and the form teacher of 1A. As a short, sharp shock, he was temporarily demoted to 1E, and then replaced in 1B. His form position in the examinations at the end of his first term was 27th out of 30 boys. In 1B he joined Clem (84). He fared no better in the B stream; his next four form positions were 2nd, 6th, 21st and then 30th. He was thus moved into the C stream, where he remained until he left the school at Easter 1965. In the C stream his academic position began to drop more sharply; 18th out of 28, 16th out of 26, 18th out of 23, 21st out of 23. Had he remained at school for the Summer Term 1965 he would probably have been demoted into 4D.

How did he become the dominant member of the delinquent group? His rise to power was a slow process. He needed to find companions with similar values, which was not possible until he had declined in the streams.

Clint used to be very quiet when he was at the other [Junior] school. He changed in second year. He began going with that gang. Then he started going up town and things like that.

He was very quiet in first year. Then in third year when he came in our class he started. Well, you see he got with all his pals in third year, the ones that he goes with nights. They was all separated when Clint and Clem were in 2B. Clem came down with Clint and Drac come up and they all got together.

Clint was pretty quiet when he first come. When Clint and me (62) went down to 3C, we started going round with Drac and then he started going round and all that, picking on little kids. Drac, you know, well he was a bit of a bighead. He's gone quiet now 'cos he's scared of Clint.

These comments are from boys who were with Clint in 1A and 1B. They will attest to the fact that Clint changed from being a fairly quiet boy, and that this change was associated with a change of friends. During the second and third years, the nucleus of the delinquent group began to take shape, especially when many of the key members found themselves in 3C. At this stage, Drac (110) dominated the group.

Drac was cock of third year. Clint wasn't a good fighter then.

It seems fully confirmed by my discussions with other boys and teachers that it was not until the third year that Clint began to assert himself, though of course the demotion from the A stream to the B stream brought him into immediate contact with Clem as reported above. Later they became two of the leading delinquent members of 4C. The change in Clint was noticed by boys in the A and B stream. As one 4A boy said:

In 1B I used to go around with Clint. He was all right. He's sensible on his own. He was on the borderline of the eleven-plus at the other school. He's clever. He could have been good at sport and all that, but he just won't go that way. It's the teachers' fault really. 'Cos he was in 1A. But because he was a bit bad they put him down into 1E. If they'd kept him in 1A and kept him clever and that, he could be cock of the school now, like, but sort of be good. Clem's another like that. He was all right in second year. I used to get on with him. It's just that when they get older they think because they can fight they have to be bigheaded. He was clever, Clem. He came near the top. He was top the term after I went into 1A. And the teacher said, 'If you're top again next term I'll put you in the A class.' He should have been put up that time. Then after that he started mixing with the bigheads and he

thought, 'If I can go down, I'll be with my friends then.'
Next term he was bottom and got put down.

The facts are correctly reported here. Clem was indeed top and
then bottom of the B stream, and thus shows a similar academic
decline to Clint. The boy who reported this was one of the most
shy members of 4A, and certainly no friend of either Clint or
Clem. That he should describe the change in attitude and behaviour in these two boys so vividly, supports the contention
that as they began to decline in the streams, and thus progressively
alienated from the staff and the academic goals of the school,
group attitudes began to take a negative turn. Life in 3C, when
Drac began to play his dominating role, marks the real beginnings
of the delinquent group.

The evidence of the duration of Drac's reign as 'cock' is
conflicting. Some boys claimed that he had been the best fighter
since the first year: others dated it only from the third year. It
appears that it took at least some two years for Drac to establish
himself in this position. The conflicting dates of origin may
result from the differential perception of his dominance, i.e. the
diffusion of the knowledge of his fighting ability spread slowly
and unevenly through his year group. And secondly, it appears
that being 'cock' does not bear any significance to members of
any one year group until the third year, when boys learn that the
fourth year has a definite cock and pecking order of fighting
ability. This explanation is intended more as a suggestion. It is
impossible to trace back the real origins; but this suggestion does
account for the conflicting reports.

Drac's reign in the third year was not permanent. Partly this
may be due to the fact that although he was a tough, wiry boy
he was also rather short, and by the third year many of his peers
were becoming very much taller and stronger than he. Secondly,
and this may be causally related to the first point, Drac's growing
self-assertiveness led to unpopularity as he began to alienate
them by his agressiveness. By the beginning of the fourth year,
when I arrived at the school, Drac had fallen into a decline of
unpopularity.

Nobody talks to Drac now. Everybody used to be scared of
him at one time. Now they stay away from him.

He was always playing dirty tricks on you. And spitting.

We fell out with Drac once when he kept beating up little kids, so we all just didn't bother with him.

Drac was hard in third year, but he's gone soft now.

Drac stopped going with me [Derek] and Clint. We didn't want him so we kept telling him to shift. And he had no one to go with except the little kids. Then some of the others started going with him.

There must have been a number of events which led to this ostracization of Drac. A typical event seems to have been:

Drac got hold of Don's towel and wiped his feet on it. He cleaned his shoes on it and so did Derek. But Derek didn't do it till after Drac. Don got him for it and beat him up and he was going to get Derek, but I don't know if he did.

Don confirmed this story.

[Drac] used to pick on everyone, worse than Clint does. Take money off them. He used to take two shillings a day off ———. And cigs and everything. He used to try and pick on me and beat me up. Then one day he got my towel and wiped his feet all over it. So I was that mad that I cracked him one. And then Clint stopped going with him so he had no one to go with. And he had to go with little kids. Then one night he got drunk and started crying that no one would go with him. So we all started going with him again and he's all right now.

It does not seem that there was any dramatic single event or fight by which Drac was replaced as 'cock'. Rather, his general unpopularity, the fact that Don did retaliate, and possibly his unwillingness to accept fights from others simply led to his decline. The ostracization of Drac, was not, so far as I was able to check, an immediate or sudden event.

But the decline of Drac marks the rise of Clint, just as later the decline of Clint coincides with the reintegration of Drac. Clint did not replace Drac by any single event. There seems to have developed some general concensus among members of the group that he was 'cock'. This process seems to have three elements. Firstly, Clint was able to spread his claim to the title on the basis of several small incidents. For example, at the end of the third year, simultaneously with Drac's decline, Clint was involved in a fight with a fourth year pupil.

He beat up a prefect last year. It was me and ———. Clint came and asked us for a penny or summat. And the prefect tried to chuck him out, you know, and Clint pushed him back like that and a fight started and Clint cut all the top of his [the prefect's] head and it started to bleed. He had to have stitches in it. Clint was hurt an' all, but he won.

This victory must have considerably enhanced Clint's claims to superior fighting ability. But this alone was insufficient to grant him the title. It does not demonstrate his ability to fight everyone else in his own year. The second element therefore is the fact that no other single boy was willing to ask Clint for a fight. This lack of challenge acted as a support for Clint's emergence. The third factor is that Clint more than any other boy made himself highly *observable* as 'hard', or tough, by a process of systematic self-display. As one A stream boy put it:

People are afraid of you if you go swaggering around the playground threatening everybody.

This is precisely what Clint did.

We can see then that the emergence of a 'cock' is not just a matter, at least prior to the fourth year, of simply displacing the reigning cock. The leadership may change by a much more subtle process. Although fighting ability is by far the most significant factor, achieving a reputation by isolated fighting events, lack of adequate challengers and self-display are important factors. By the end of first term of the fourth year, Clint had fully established his reputation. This was clear from my attempts to find out *how* Clint had become cock of the school. He himself was very uninformative about the matter, but others came to my aid.

I don't know *how*. It's just the way you act really. It's just their reputation, if you know what I mean. Like Clint. It's not because he's fought everybody in the school. It's just the reputation. He can probably fight Don, so the rest think he can fight them.

It's just got round that Clint is the best fighter. But you don't know really 'cos they've never had him a fight.

Clint must be the best fighter 'cos he can beat Don and he can fight Clem too. Everyone says so.

Don of 4D was generally agreed to be 'second cock'. The next four or five positions were not sharply defined. Everyone knew the names of the boys occupying these ranks, but the actual order was not agreed. This was because the boys were friends; the fights by which definite positions could be determined did not take place. Although fighting ability was a major criterion of informal status in the delinquent group it was not the only one. Don, the 'second cock' held informal status rank 5 in 4D. This is because high informal status is partly determined by closeness to Clint. As we shall see, Don was not well-disposed to Clint, and was somewhat ambivalent in his relationship with him. Derek of 4D was Clint's closest friend, and it was Derek who held the top informal status rank in 4D. Even though Derek was not one of the five best fighters in the fourth year, his close friendship with Clint granted him high *associated status*.

Changes in the 'pecking order' can, however, occur when one boy offers to fight another. If the superior fighter declines to accept a challenge, the two boys change ranks. If he accepts, a fight ensues, and the winner obtains the higher rank. Likewise, if the leader or 'cock' feels in danger of being replaced, he can forestall the potential threat to his position by asking the challenger for a fight. Drac had done this in the third year.

Clem came into our class. He should have been cock, him. I asked him for a fight but he wouldn't have one.

In this way Drac anticipated and defeated a rebellion before it could take place. And similarly, Clint maintained his superiority over Don, his nearest potential rival.

Clint must be the best fighter 'cos Don won't have him a scrap. Clint's the best fighter. Then Don comes next. They've never had a fight, but Clint's the best fighter 'cos Don won't have him.

Yet Don was not scared of Clint, and was *known* not to be afraid.

Everyone's scared of Clint, but I don't think Don is.

And this fact was known to Clint. He no longer tried to be very aggressive towards Don, who pointed out:

> Clint's changed now. You couldn't say nothing to him then [in the third year], you know what I mean? He'd turn round and crack you, but now he's all right.

But at the same time, Don did not want to challenge Clint.

> I don't want a fight with Clint. 'Cos if he beat me he'd be a big hero, like, wouldn't he? And I wouldn't want to beat him. 'Cos then I'd be first and I wouldn't like that.

This remark looks superficially like a justification of cowardice. This is not so. Don was very popular among the boys, and was frequently compared with Clint.

> Don's better to get on with. He doesn't know whether he can beat Clint. He'd have a good go though. No one else could have a go.

> I wish Don would beat Clint. 'Cos he's not a bighead. He's not always going round beating people up.

> [If Clint and Don had a fight] it might be a close fight that. 'Cos Don's a good scrapper. It might be a draw, I don't know. But I think Don would put up a good fight if he had to take him on. Clem says he won't have him a fight.

> Don's smashing to get on with. You've no need to be frightened of him 'cos he won't touch you.

> Don's about the best one. He never bothers anybody. But he's not frightened of anybody in the school. He acts more like a grown up, does Don. If he's got some toffees he gives you some, but the rest won't hand none out. But they expect you to hand yours out.

Don was indeed a much more mature boy than Clint. He commanded loyalty from other boys and became popular because his fighting ability was not used to dominate. Moreover, he was able to see, as shown in the earlier quotation, that becoming 'cock' would endanger this popularity. On numerous occasions he seems to have been tempted to fight Clint, both for his own self-esteem and in order to 'tame' Clint. But his fear of becoming an unpopular 'cock' restrained him. It is not that unpopularity is inherent in the position of 'cock'. The 'cock' is of high informal status because of the power he is able to exert over others, even against their will. 'Popularity' is a different dimension which is concerned with personal preference and the ability to elicit and maintain sympathetic relationships. Don was more popular than Clint; he received eleven choices from 4C and 4D boys on the 'friends' question, whereas Clint received only six. It seems that to maintain fully his position as 'cock' the occupant must combine high status in terms of both power and popularity, even though power is the primary prerequisite. That is, the 'cock' must *legitimate* his authority in that the followers accept him not only because he can force his will upon them, but also because they willingly consent to his exercise of power because they like him. The fusion of these two dimensions of power and popularity was no mean task for the reigning 'cock'. The potential risk of unpopularity in being 'cock' was explained clearly by Drac, who in describing Clint elucidates his own failure to acquire popularity as 'cock'.

> I'm glad I'm not cock now. You know, they don't seem to like you when you're cock of the school. They don't like Clint now 'cos he's a bighead 'cos he's cock. They all say Don will be able to fight him, so Don's waiting for him to start on him but he hasn't said owt to him yet. If he says owt to Don, Don's going to get him. Clint thinks he's friends with him, but Don doesn't like him. He's too bigheaded, you know. Some little kids come up to him and he cracks them and everything. But Don, you know, all the little kids can punch him, you know, act the goat with him, but he won't do owt.

Clint, by his indiscriminate aggression, began to follow the same fate as Drac and lost the support of his followers.

> Everyone knows Clint 'cos he's cock, but he's not popular, 'cos no one likes him, you know what I mean? I don't see why he should go round bullying people like he does just 'cos you can fight them. Taking money off them and all that. He's bigheaded.
>
> (Don)

I liked Clint more in third year. Now he seems to be jumping on everybody, you know, and putting them on the floor and all that. And hitting them. I've seen him kick people in the face and start his nose bleeding.

They're all frightened of Clint. I used to go with him for about two years, but then I stopped going with him 'cos he nutted me.

I don't like Clint much now. He's got too bigheaded. And he was dead mad when I started talking to Drac again.

(Clem)

You can't tell with Clint. One minute he's talking with you and then the next minute he's saying 'Shut up'. He's like that all the time.

All these comments are from members of the delinquent group taken in the second half of the Spring Term. The same trend is followed by Chris (67) his reciprocated first choice on the sociogram (Chart III). The two boys always sat in adjacent seats for a term and a half. When this ceased, Chris explained:

I don't like him much now. He's always messing around. He's all right outside school but I don't like him in school. He asked me to sit next to him when we first come in this class. But I didn't really know him and he didn't know me. I liked him for a time. But then he began messing around and doing things, you know, so I just moved away. I said, 'I'm just going sitting somewhere else near the radiator 'cos it's cold,' and then I stayed there. He's been more friendly since I stopped sitting next to him.

Up to this point the stress in the description has been on the conflicts and instability of the group. This emphasis, while essential to a full analysis of the group, fails to give adequate weight to the co-operative and integrative activities of the group, which could be daily observed, especially during lessons. One further example would be the 'extortion racket', which followed in the Drac tradition. All non-members of the group were potential victims.

Like Derek, he came up to me and said, 'Lend us a penny.' I said, 'What for?' He said, 'To go to't Cavern.' I said, 'No' but he didn't bother and he turned to [my friend] and showed him 1/5d and said, 'Look I've cadged this today.'

Clint lets you off if you've only got a penny like and you need it for your bus fare or summat. But if you've got any more he'll take some. He might even take half. And if you don't pay you get smashed.

They say, 'Have you got a penny?' And if you say, 'No' they search your pockets. They search your pockets and you can't do nowt.

Membership of the group thus had a protective function: it insulated a boy against aggressive attacks and extortion. But not all the group members were involved in extortion. Don was a notable exception, and this fact may have contributed to his loss of informal status, and an increase in his general popularity.

The majority of the delinquent group had a Court record and were involved in current petty crime. Many of the accounts are very similar to those reported by members of 4B, such as the *collective* nature of the commission of the crimes. But there are important differences. In the B stream the main form of theft is incidental and petty. Cigarettes, sweets, cakes, minerals and small trinkets from multiple stores are the most common of the articles stolen. Although this also occurred in the delinquent group, there are important differences. Firstly, criminality is more purposeful and organized. Rather than taking place, as was the case in 4B, 'on the way', on an incidental basis, it is planned before hand and often a special journey into the town is made. And when the boys get there, they arrange more carefully who will play which role.

I generally go with someone else. You wouldn't go on your own, not up town. They suspect you more if you're on your own. If you're on your own you can't just pick them up and put them in your pocket 'cos you don't know who's watching. But when there's two of you one can just walk round and look who's there. You go in separately and meet again when you come out.

They learn by experience which shops are 'easier' than others.

I've nicked lots of small things out of Woolworths. The last few Saturdays I been down to town with them. But I must stop going with them. I had all the stuff on me. Like ———, he had all those stolen records in a bag and the floorwalker – I know her – she started to follow him. But if they'd caught me I'd have got done. I told them when they were in this cafe that she was following us.

They won't let you in ———'s now. They keep their eye on them with long hair. A bit ago they used to leave all the records on the counter and you could easily shove them up your jacket.

———'s is supposed to be the hardest place; they prosecute.

In addition, the quality of the stolen articles tends to increase in price. Clothes – significantly – become a major item of interest. This is perhaps partly because the home fails to provide them and partly because of pressures to be fashionable.

Shirts from up town. You just pretend you're looking at them like that then you drop two on the floor and as you're picking one up you put one down your pants. A mate of mine just put a jacket with a leather collar on, took the tab off, and just walked out. No one stopped him.

———'s nicked everything he's got on. His pants, his corduroy jumper, his shirt and all that. He spends the money his mam gives him and then tells her he's bought the clothes.

I folded two pair of pants up and went into the changing room, wrapped one pair round my waist and took the other pair back. Then I put my jacket on and put my coat over it and just walked away.

In 4B I could find little evidence of acts of 'malicious damage', a common element of delinquency, though I am certain that it did take place on a limited scale. In the delinquent group such acts were fairly common.

We were once near the canal and there was this big boat. I was going to push it in but it was dead heavy. A big canoe sort of. And it fit thirty odd people. So we shoved it in the canal and it turned over. A bloke run and phoned the cops and they all came so we jumped on the boat and got across. About four of us got away. We was hiding in this grass, but ——— got caught.

Last night ———— got this tin and went like that and threw it through this window. Then we ran away.

Once when we was going by the chip shop ———— kicked a window and it went in. So he ran out and I was the last one and the others were all in front so he just got hold of my coat like that and I just hit his hand and let go.

Sometimes when trains came past we'd throw stones at the windows. Me and ————, we got stopped by this plain-clothes copper, he got hold of ———— and me and took us in this car, and he didn't get our names until we was in the car. I wanted to run away but we couldn't. I had to go to Court. Another mate of mine used to climb up the signals and make dents in them with a brick, you know. We got done for that as well and we had to pay £4.

I found that whilst many of the boys were happy to discuss their various thefts, they were curiously reticent about acts of malicious damage. It was as if they felt some shame about such gratuitously destructive behaviour. Two boys told me that they thought the majority of the delinquent group were involved in such acts but they thought that some were simply afraid to tell me about it. Another frequent misdemeanour was to obtain entry to a cinema secretly without paying:

You open the toilet doors and pretend you've been in. Or you can get in from the outside doors. You've only got to get a piece of wire in the door and pull it. At the ———— you open the door, go up some stairs, and just before the screen there's a curtain. Well, you've got to crawl on the floor by this curtain and get into a seat. They got ———— the other day just as he was getting into a seat.

Of course, some of these boys were able liars and would be completely unscrupulous in avoiding blame and guilt.

I'm always the one that gets caught. I got done nicking some mouth organs. He asked my name so I told him another lad's name. He's in a home now. He stole £170 from a pub.

The delinquent group contrasts with the B stream boys in that only from the former did I find frequent attempts to rationalize their delinquency.

You see kids pinching off the milk cart. It's natural. They can't help it. Some people deserve it though. You go in one shop and they have things all over the counter.

It's not wrong to nick things out of shops. They've got more money than us.

But they were not complete fools: they knew how the dice were loaded against them and played the game accordingly. They relied on the fact that firms caution more often than they prosecute.

Once I leave school and start work I'm going to be dead careful. 'Cos if you get caught then, you go into court and get done. When you're at school it's a matter of you can get done or you can't get done. That's why a lot of lads do pinch. You see more kids at school pinching than grown ups or owt like that.

And of course the drama of delinquency, for all its dangers, had a romantic aspect which gave identification with gangsters and commanded the attention of the group.

They took us to this cop-shop and it was just like a gaol. You know, there were all bars and they kept locking all the doors. We was like real convicts.

The home atmosphere of some members of the delinquent group seems to have been more permissive than of boys in higher streams (See Chapter Seven). In such cases, the home acts as a reinforcer of the group norms.

I only swipe cigs off my dad. If he catches me he just tells me to put them back.

My dad caught me smoking once. He comes in and I was sitting in this chair. He was going to batter me but my mam says, 'Oh, they all do it so why shouldn't he?' My mam gives me cigs, sometimes.

(Clem)

But Clem also reports that his parents were not permissive about drink.

I went home drunk the other week. Well, I wasn't exactly

drunk, you know, it had wore off. But my face was all red. And she wanted to know what I'd had and she found out and she went to the pub for my dad and he come out and kept me in.

One boy in 4D was taken to Court for taking a motor-bike without the owner's consent, with the additional charges for driving without a licence and insurance, etc. The police visited the parents, and when the police had gone the father's first re-mark to his son, as it was reported to me, was:

Hadn't you got the bloody sense to dump it?

The father was not concerned about the delinquent act *per se*, but its unintelligent commission.

But let us be clear on this point. I am not claiming that from the evidence of this study that the delinquent group members come from homes which are more supportive of a delinquent sub-culture – though such may be the case. The evidence about home background in this study is extremely slight. Rather, there is *some* indication that *some* of the delinquent group come from homes which seem supportive of criminal tendencies, especially since some of them had fathers and brothers with prison records. But this was also true for some of the non-delinquent members of higher streams. The point here is that the relation between home background and delinquency is not simple, and cannot by itself provide an adequate explanation. The present argument is making an obvious point: that where the home is less orientated against criminal tendencies, entry in to the delinquent group and an acceptance of its norms will be considerably facilitated.

Our central concern is with the informal processes in the group and the pressures it mediates. The forces exerted by the delin-quent group on its members are difficult to detect, since many of the key situations were not open to observation. But a number of examples are available.

On Saturday, 64 says to 70, 'Have a cig.' He says, 'No.' So he says, 'If you don't have a cig you don't come round with us no more.' So he says, 'Right give us a cig.'

Here the group exerts pressure on a boy to practise a behaviour which is proscribed by home and school alike. Unless he conforms to the group he will be rejected. Even if on such an occasion a boy is not threatened with direct rejection, he will be teased or scorned for being 'soft', an effective taunt for bringing deviants into line with group practices.

98, an aspirant, that is unreciprocated, member of the A clique in 4D became increasingly unpopular with the staff during his last year at school. He was regarded as having become very 'silly' and 'stupid'. The boy was aware of it himself. In his own words:

I'm more cheeky now. I used to be dead quiet when I first come.

He had learned that being quiet did not earn recognition from the group: he needed to be visibly and actively conformist to the norms of the group.

98 goes round slapping kids necks. He's mad, him.

98's gone bigheaded. It's only 'cos he thinks he's started to be one of the cocks of the school.

To be seen to be conforming thus requires a boy to *over*-conform to some extent. And the kind of behaviour which is practised can only be learned from imitation of the boys with high status. Let us consider the boy of status rank 14 in 4D.

When I first come, well they thought I was dead quiet, never giving cheek and they used to pick on me but when I started giving cheek they started treating me like anyone else.

This is the *negative* side of the process by which the group punishes the boy since he refuses to conform. This is followed by the *positive* side by which the boy begins to acquire the norms of the group and demonstrate them behaviourally. He continues:

When I heard Don answering back [to the teachers], you know, then I got started. Once I got six slippers for answering back. He [the teacher] told me to come back after dinner. And I had to do a test and he said, 'If it's not finished you'll have to do it at 4 o'clock', but I didn't go back and he says, 'Why didn't you come back?' and I said, "Cos I din't want to', and I said I couldn't and then he gave me four and says 'I hope this'll refresh your memory', and I said, 'Get lost', and he hit me again.

In this way a boy can change his concept of the pupil role to conformity to group expectations but to deviance from teacher expectations. Because the group rewards him more than the teachers do, the group norms become more attractive than those of the teacher.

It will be evident that the delinquent group would frequently be involved in conflict with the teachers. On a number of occasions the incompatibility between teacher expectations and group norms was made quite explicit. We shall consider two examples.

The first took place on the last day of the Easter Term when most of the delinquent group were leaving school. On a number of occasions two members of the group had told me what they intended to do to certain of the less popular teachers as their Parthian dart to the system. I regarded these as verbal outlets for their aggression, and assumed that none of them would materialize on the day. None of these plans did: but another plan was accepted.

All the boys in the group bought fresh eggs during the lunch hour. These were concealed in their pockets during the last afternoon when boys are allowed to play records and games with their form teachers. On these eggs the boys drew pictures of a particular master at whom these eggs were to be thrown after the final Assembly. However, one teacher spotted one of the eggs and confiscated it. On observing that one teacher's nickname was written on it, he quickly guessed the purpose of the eggs and informed the Headmaster, who then summoned all the leavers into the Hall. He had questioned the boy who was found with the egg in his possession, Chris and also Clint and two of his main followers, 62 and 79. His attempts to extract the truth from these boys, met of course, with complete failure. The Head upbraided the whole fourth year about the danger of making such protests and warned them that they would not be given their Leaving Certificates until after the final Assembly and told them (falsely) that without these Leaving Certificates they would be unable to get a National Insurance Card or a job. Anyone who showed the slightest sign of misbehaviour would be refused a Certificate. The plot was thus foiled, but the hostility towards the teacher who was the object of the scheme was increased. As soon as the boys received their Certificates, they

rushed out of school, armed with some of the remaining eggs
and other missiles and waited for the teacher to drive his car off
the school premises. Fortunately for the teacher, he was able to
avoid the crowd of some fifty or sixty boys awaiting him.

The second illustration is much more illuminating, in that it
represents not one isolated event, but a continuous clash between
the standards the teachers wish to impose and the norms of the
delinquent group.

At the time of the study many of the 'pop' groups playing 'beat'
music had long hair styles – the Beatles, the Rolling Stones, the
Kinks and so on. Throughout the town many teenage boys
imitated these styles. It is not surprising, therefore, that at the
beginning of the Autumn Term 1964 a few boys in the fourth
year arrived at school with long hair. The origin of this fashion,
which by the middle of the fourth year had spread to many
high status boys in the B stream, was in the delinquent group.

Clint says, 'I'm going to get my hair flicking up', so I says,
'I'm going to let mine grow too', so he says, 'O.K.' So then
we started letting it grow and then everyone did.

(Derek)

There was only three of us grew it long at first. There was me,
Clint and Derek. But 105 had his hair long before it come out
in fashion, I think. I just grew mine long but they thought
they'd look hard if they didn't have it cut.

(112)

I wasn't going to grow it long at first and then they all said,
'Are you going to get your hair cut?' so I let it grow long.
I'd rather have it short now but I'm not going to get it cut.
I'd look a right nit.

Many of the older boys had been wearing jeans in school for
some time and the staff had made regular but not entirely successful attempts to ban jeans in school. Although the Headmaster
was aware that the Local Education Authority would not support
his refusal to accept a boy in school because of wearing jeans, he
announced in Assembly that jeans were against the school rules.
This rule was strongly resented by many boys for several reasons.
Several other schools in the area did not enforce rules against
jeans at school. Some felt that when the fashionable narrow

trousers were worn at school they tended to become shapeless very quickly. Also some boys possessed only one pair of trousers and wished to keep these as a 'best' pair.

A few days after the beginning of the Autumn Term, the Deputy-Headmaster called the top four informal status boys of 4D out of their classroom and told them that he would not tolerate this flouting of the school rules and that in future they must wear trousers to school. He explained to me afterwards that he hoped in this way to nip this incipient revolt in the bud. Yet the wearing of jeans continued intermittently, so a few weeks later one of the teachers asked for guidance on this matter at a Staff Meeting. The Headmaster pointed out that they could expect no support from the L.E.A. for their policy, and that the staff must therefore use informal sanctions against the wearing of jeans. All privileges would be withheld from offending pupils. One teacher pointed out that the offending pupils were the ones who in any case did not want privileges. The Head teacher retracted his remarks and stated that a boy must not be penalized simply because he wore jeans at school.

Many of the staff were not satisfied by this. Lengthy, informal discussions took place in the Staff Room and over lunch. The most vociferous members of staff were strongly opposed to jeans and long hair, and expressed their opinion in no uncertain terms. They argued that long hair was unhygienic and encouraged the spread of lice in the school; that it was dangerous, especially in the school workshops; that it was very unsightly and effeminate.[3]

By November, when a second Staff Meeting was held, many tempers had been roused. As a result the Headmaster authorized the use of informal sanctions against the offenders. They were to be excluded from participation in the school concert, and from school visits. He also said, 'They'll get no help from me and I shan't give them a reference when they leave.' One of the teachers strongly objected to this policy, arguing that the academic development of the children was the school's real function, not the determination of styles of dress. No other teacher supported this objection, though one teacher expressed his agreement to me privately. The Deputy Headmaster countered the objection with a justification of the policy on the grounds that these boys were in any case disobeying their parents by having long hair and jeans and that the boys concerned were simply trying to be awkward in school. It was suggested that a long-haired member of 2A should be transferred to the E stream 'as an example' but this was not in fact carried out.

The more general policy was put into effect. Boys with long hair or jeans were excluded from school visits, though this affected very few boys since only 4A and 4B were involved in these visits. The few offenders in these upper streams tended to capitulate and conform to teacher expectations as the year progressed. (One persistent deviant in 4A stayed at school for a fifth year, but since one master refused to teach him unless he had his hair cut, he left a few weeks after the beginning of his fifth year.) Teachers constantly made adverse and derogatory remarks about long hair and jeans. Such comments usually took the form of ridicule or an attempt to shame the pupils for their 'scruffy' appearance. Most of the teachers seemed almost completely unaware that such pressures would be unavailing since group norms were much more attractive and compelling than teacher expectations.

At the end of the Autumn Term the local Inspector of Schools attended the school's Carol Service, and criticized the appearance of many boys. This caused the Headmaster to instigate a sort of 'purge' on jeans and long hair, and on lack of cleanliness, which he tended to see as synonymous. In an announcement to the whole school he said that boys who came to school in a dirty state in the Spring Term would be sent to the Chief Education Officer with a note to the effect that he, the Headmaster, would not accept these boys in school until they were more presentable. He also repeated that those boys with long hair could not expect a reference from him when they left school. He stated publicly that offenders would be excluded from extra-curricular activities. Finally he indicated that such boys would experience great difficulty in finding an employer when they left school.

At lunch that day a heated discussion ensued amongst the teachers. The majority agreed that long hair was a sign of anti-social behaviour and must be stamped out. Two teachers thought that long hair was a part of an adolescent phase and bore little relevance to the teacher's function.

The Spring Term marked the beginning of concerted opposition to jeans and long hair. On the first day of term boys with jeans were excluded from Assembly and lectured about the matter. One fourth year teacher openly admitted that he had caned six boys for having hair over their eyes and would continue to do so daily until they had it cut. The application of informal sanctions continued. The Headmaster wrote on one boy's report to the Youth Employment Officer, 'Has long hair.' The Headmaster refused to let boys with long hair have time off school to visit their future employers. He told the low stream. boys:

> Make yourself look normal. Make your appearance normal, instead of being like nothing on earth, or you'll not get a job. If an employer has two lads to choose from, he'll pick the normal one, not you.

One teacher began cutting the hair of these pupils, an act which caused considerable dismay amongst the boys. The teacher did not, perhaps significantly, cut the hair of the leaders of the delinquent group, but of low status boys. However, one irate parent complained to the Education Offices about this, and the matter was hastily hushed up. The less drastic pressures continued. Bert of 4B was not allowed to sell flags in a local cinema for charity because the Headmaster considered that the boy's appearance would give an unfavourable impression of the school. It was on these grounds that several high status low stream boys were forbidden to attend the Leavers' Service at a local Church at the end of the Spring Term.

The teachers who disagreed with the Headmaster's policy formed a very small minority. One part-time teacher spontaneously told me that he disagreed with the policy for two reasons: firstly, the rule against jeans and long hair provided a means for the boys to express their antagonism to the system; secondly, the rule was arbitrary, since dirty trousers were considered more acceptable than clean jeans. Other teachers would not follow this argument.

As a researcher I tried to avoid becoming involved in the argument, but when my opinion was asked I felt it best to be honest and express my disagreement with the Headmaster's policy. I pointed out that when I had visited a local beat club with some of the boys I had felt very uncomfortable and out of place because of my *short* hair. On these grounds, we should appreciate that the club was more attractive to these boys than school, so we could not expect to win. Secondly, although I agreed that it was part of the teacher's duty to make the boys clean and tidy, I did not feel it was part of the school's function to dictate styles of dress. Thirdly, I stated that the Headmaster had informed me, after a visit from the school nurse, that with exceptions it was not the boys with long hair who tended to carry lice, since they washed their hair frequently. Finally, I suggested that long hair was perhaps a symbol of the boys' rejection of the school's values and that our opposition would only exacerbate this rejection. These arguments were hotly refuted by many teachers who were present.

Conflict between staff and boys continued. The Deputy Headmaster refused to consider Don for appointment as a prefect because of his long hair, despite support for his candidature from several teachers. As one teacher said:

> I don't care a damn over his long hair, but if that's the school policy it's O.K. by me.

One boy in 4C who was an aspirant member of Clint's group, was offered ten shillings by his mother and the same amount from his grandmother to have his hair cut short. His refusal in spite of these incentives is an interesting index of the symbolic importance of long hair in aligning him so visibly with the delinquent group.

Most of the delinquent group were leaving school at Easter. Few of them made any real attempt to secure employment. Part of this was their reluctance to have their hair cut. One boy in 4C did have his cut prior to an interview with a prospective employer a few days before the end of term. He was, of course, excessively teased by both teachers and peers. Derek had his hair cut short on the evening after he left school. He was not willing, one might infer, to let teachers or pupils see that he was willing to abandon his long hair in order to get a job. He maintained his opposition to the last.

Chapter Seven

OUT OF SCHOOL

The main purpose of this study is to examine the relationships of boys in school in terms of formal and informal organization. Hitherto we have shown how boys in the fourth year at Lumley are differentiated along a number of dimensions. Is this reflected in their behaviour outside school? To separate life inside school from life outside school would be somewhat arbitrary, as our analysis of the delinquent group disclosed: there is no clear line of distinction. Because behaviour is not neatly divided into segments, we shall in this section examine some selected aspects of behaviour which, although not central to our thesis, may reflect processes occurring in school. Boys import values and attitudes from their families and friends which influence life in school. But this is a two-way process. What they do in school, what values they acquire, what norms they conform to, all these affect behaviour outside the confines of the school building.

At no stage was it intended to unravel the complex set of inter-relations which exist between home and school. A number of other studies have appeared, or are currently being undertaken, to investigate this problem. For this reason the study was pur-posely limited to analysis of the dynamic processes at work *within* the school. There was thus no direct investigation of the influence of home background: homes were not visited, nor were parents interviewed. Such factors, however, are essential to a fuller understanding of the life of children in school, so we shall present the reader with the little information that is available on the Lumley boys.

Many sociologists have been concerned to show the relation between 'social class' of the family, as defined by the father's occupation, and the child's academic attainment or selection for Grammar Schools. Jackson has also demonstrated the close relation between social class and stream level in primary schools.

The relevant figures for Lumley Secondary Modern School are given in Tables XXVIII and XXIX. Of the 53 per cent of the boys who came from Class III or above homes, 94 per cent have fathers in skilled manual occupations; less than six per cent of the fathers have non-manual jobs. Semi-skilled (Class IV) and unskilled (Class V) occupations account for almost a further

TABLE XXVIII

Social Class Distribution (By year group)

Year	% Class III and above	% Class IV	% Class V	% No father or father unemployed	Not classi- fied %	N
1st	57	12	19	8	4	97
2nd	52	15	20	11	2	119
3rd	52	16	23	8	1	111
4th	52	22	16	9	1	122
All	53	17	19	9	2	449

20 per cent each, and almost 10 per cent of the boys have fathers who are dead, separated or unemployed. The variations between each year group are extremely small. When we consider streams, we note a *slight* tendency, which is not statistically significant, for the higher streams to have a disproportionate number of fathers from Class III occupations. The one marked trend in Table XXIX is for the E stream boys to come from homes where father is unemployed or where there is no father at all. We may conclude that the streaming system at Lumley does not reflect, in any striking form, selection by social class.[1]

The most detailed study of the relation between home and school based on British children is that of Douglas and his associates.[2] Douglas did not use the Registrar-General's system of social class divisions, but devised a system based on parent's level of education. In this way he was able to divide the 'working

TABLE XXIX

Social Class Distribution (By stream)

Stream	% Class III and above	% Class IV	% Class V	% No father or father unemployed	Not classified %	N
A	62	17	16	4	1	112
B	51	19	22	7	1	100
C	53	13	22	10	2	92
D	49	21	24	5	1	78
E	48	13	12	22	5	67
All	53	17	19	9	2	449

class' population, which includes the boys at Lumley, into an 'upper' and a 'lower' section. He was able to demonstrate that not only are working class children differentiated from middle class children along a number of important dimensions, including educational ones, but his measures also distinguished between the upper and lower working class. The upper section is superior to the lower in terms of the average test scores of the children, the standards of care provided by the home, the parental desire for Grammar School education, the age at which the parents desired the child to leave school, the extent of parental interest in the child's progress at school, and so on.

Douglas used over five thousand children in his sample and on this basis is able to make reasonably firm generalizations. The boys in their fourth year at Lumley number just over a hundred. At the same time we may consider some selected factors which have been shown to differentiate between homes. Table XXX gives the figures for the average family size of pupils in each stream of the fourth year. Every other year group at Lumley shows the same trend: the higher the stream, the smaller the average family size.[3] This is similar to the finding of Douglas

TABLE XXX

Family Size and Bedrooms

Form	Mean Family size (Children only)	Mean Number of Bedrooms per household	Mean Number of Children per Bedroom*
4A	3·17	2·50	2·14
4B	3·76	2·36	2·87
4C	4·05	2·40	2·87
4D	4·45	2·68	2·65
All Forms	3·90	2·50	2·60
D-Group	4·87	2·48	3·29
Rest	3·57	2·57	2·27
D-Group & Rest	4·25	2·52	2·79

* Excluding one bedroom for parents.

that as the families increase in size, the test score delines, even when social class is kept constant.

The average number of bedrooms per family is almost the same for each stream, which can be predicted from our knowledge that the homes from which the Lumley boys come are basically of the same size and design. From the combination of family size and bedrooms we can calculate an index of overcrowding, that is, the number of children per bedroom. It is clear that as we descend the streams, the extent of this overcrowding increases. We may thus conclude that the higher the stream, the smaller the family size and the less the extent of overcrowding tends to be.

We may note too, that if we separate the delinquent group from the remaining members of 4C and 4D, the members of the delinquent group tend to come from homes with a higher average number of children and thus with a greater degree of over-crowding.[4] This may, in part, account for the delinquent group members' tendency to spend less of their leisure time at home than any other group of Lumley boys (See below).

These are crude indices. In order to attempt to differentiate between pupils' homes without actually visiting the parents, a questionnaire was administered to each boy consisting of questions designed to elicit information on the physical attributes of

TABLE XXXI

Home Status

Dimension	% Qualifying				
	4A	4B	4C	4D	*All*
Owns Present House	29	29	11	15	24
Hot-water system (all forms)	57	76	79	70	69
Fixed Fire in 'Back' Room	75	62	50	81	68
Indoor Lavatory	14	19	21	15	17
Bathroom	35	38	37	35	36
Washing Machine	63	68	64	70	65
Refrigerator	16	25	0	22	16
Car	30	18	14	17	20

the home. The vast majority of these items failed to differentiate between streams, as would perhaps be expected from the general uniformity of the housing in the area. A sample of these items is presented in Table XXXI, from which it can be seen that no clear pattern emerges. In only two cases are there indications of differentiation between streams. Boys in 4A and 4B come from homes which are more frequently owned rather than rented than is the case in 4C and 4D; and the parents of A boys seem to own a car more often than others. Whilst there are few indications of differences between streams we may note the general information on home status, such as the small number of homes with an indoor lavatory.

A less objective estimate of home background can be obtained by asking children to describe the attitudes of their parents in a number of areas. Each child was presented with a questionnaire (Q.13) which forced a choice between three alternatives of parental attitude: the boy was asked to indicate which of the three was closest to the attitude of his parents. Three of these – the extent of parental attempted control over choice of friends, over the purchase of clothes, and the parents' reaction to late arrival at home in the evening – failed to provide statistically significant differences between streams. This last of the three questions was expected to show differences since when boys were asked to state their average time of going to bed, the figures are, 10.25 p.m., 10.35, 10.39 and 11.05 for the A, B, C and D streams respectively. The other five areas of parental attitude (See Table XXXII) do produce statistically significant differences between streams. We may summarize them by saying, the higher the stream, the greater the tendency for parents to:

—seek a job for the son which is 'superior' to his father's.

—be more severe in their attitude to low academic achievement.

—be less permissive about smoking.

—require the child to do jobs at home.

—take the child with them for leisure purposes outside the home.

The question on parental reaction to low academic achievement in the child, albeit an inadequate one, may be one way in which we can confirm Douglas's finding that the test scores declined as the family became larger and the level of parental interest decreased. He was also able to show, since his sample was large, that parental interest waned as family size increased. In our small sample, we may note that for boys in the lower streams, the family size tends to be larger and the parents seem less concerned about level of academic achievement.

The first question, concerning the parents' wishes about the occupational choice of the son, is not an easy one to interpret, since it does not take into account the actual level of father's occupation. This factor does not however, appear to influence

TABLE XXXII
Indicators of Parental Attitudes

Dimension	Trend	Statistical Test (Chi-Square)
Q. i. Wishing child to have a better job than father's.	Higher the stream, the greater the desire.	P < ·01
Q. ii. Parents' control over child's friends.	Most parents seek high control.	Not sig.
Q. iii. Parents' reaction to low academic achievement.	Higher the stream, the more severe the parents' reaction.	P < ·025
Q. iv. Parents' views on child's smoking.	Higher the stream, the less permissive the parents.	P < ·025
Q. v. Parents' control over the buying of child's clothes.	Most parents allow freedom of choice.	Not sig.
Q. vi. Parents' expectation that child will do jobs at home.	The higher the stream, the more often child does jobs at home.	P < ·05
Q. vii. Going out with parents for leisure purposes.	Higher the stream, the more often the child goes out with parents.	P < ·005
Q. viii. Parents' reaction to child's coming home late at night.	Most parents moderately severe.	Not sig.

the parents' aspirations for the son, since of all those with fathers in Class III, 53 per cent say their parents wish them to have a better job than father, and 51 per cent of those with Class IV or Class V fathers make the same claim. It thus appears that the actual level of father's occupation does not affect the result. The reason for this is perhaps that no specific occupations were indicated; the boy is simply reporting his feeling that his parents wish him to 'get on', that is, to get further in the world than father did. If this is the case, then the question is a measure of parents' general interest in the boy's future. This is found to be related to stream: the percentage of boys claiming that their parents wish them to have a better job than father's are 71, 64, 46 and 21 for 4A, 4B, 4C and 4D respectively. The same trend is observable in Table XXXIII where the boys' *own* occupational aspirations are similarly stream-related.

TABLE XXXIII

Occupational Aspiration

Form	% Desiring Non-manual or skilled job	% Desiring semi- or unskilled job	N
4A	93	7	30
4B	64	36	28
4C	55	45	22
4D	41	59	22
All	67	33	102

Chi-square = 17·40   D.f. = 3   P<·001

Information was also collected on whether or not the mother was employed. The results in Table XXXIV show that 63 per cent of the mothers had some sort of job, though nearly two thirds of these are on a part-time basis. There are indications of a slight tendency for the proportion of boys with working mothers to increase as we descend the streams. We may also note

TABLE XXXIV

Working Mothers

Form	Part-time and full-time %	Part-time %	Full-time %
4A	53	23	30
4B	68	57	11
4C	65	39	26
4D	70	39	30
All	63	39	24

that 72 per cent of the mothers of the delinquent group have jobs, whereas the figure for the rest of 4C and 4D is 59 per cent. But this difference is very slight with such a small sample of boys, and cannot be taken to indicate that delinquency is associated with working mothers, especially when some studies have shown this to be untrue.[5]

The data examined in this chapter cannot by any means be regarded as an adequate discussion of the relation between home and school, especially when we consider that some of the evidence on parental attitudes has been derived from the boys, rather than the parents themselves. Yet it does provide evidence which is in line with other researches. Although these families cannot be differentiated in terms of the physical attributes or amenities of the home, there is a tendency for boys in the higher streams to come from homes where the family size is smaller with a consequent decrease in overcrowding. More significantly, there is some indirect evidence that the parental attitudes of high stream boys, especially in respect of occupational aspiration and encouragement of academic achievement, are more orientated to the values of the school and its teachers.

This study must confess its limitations; it has omitted the major variable of the home, without which our knowledge of the influence of school is incomplete. Douglas, in noting the close relationship between the child's attitude to work at school and the level of the parental encouragement writes:

> When the children are divided into those who 'work hard or very hard', who are 'average', or who are 'poor workers or lazy', in each group the average test score made at eleven years increases in passing from those whose parents take little interest in their work to those whose parents take much interest; but less so than when no account is taken of the children's attitude to their school work. When one looks, not at the level of test scores, but at the changes in average score between eight and eleven years, the level of interest of parents has negligible effect and the attitude of the children towards their work a considerable one. The hard-working children improve their scores on the average between eight and eleven years whether their parents encourage them or not, and the poor workers and lazy children deteriorate in performance whatever their parents' attitude . . .[6]

There comes a point, as Douglas indicates, where the influence of home ceases or becomes weak; this is the point at which peer group influences begin to assert themselves. Studies of the relative influence of home and school are few, though one American study has shown that college aspiration in high school pupils is more a function of peer group influence than of home by the senior year, whereas the reverse is true at the freshman stage.[7] It is these influences, the informal pressures towards conformity, that this study is concerned to reveal. Home may be supportive of the school, especially when it meets no opposition in the peer group. We find that at Lumley 4A boys come from homes which are less permissive about smoking and that this is reinforced by the academic orientation of the informal group, resulting in a low amount of actual smoking and disapproval of such behaviour. But a boy with such a home background in the lower streams finds himself in conflict with the dominant peer group norms, and conformity to home and teachers requires the assumption of low informal status. Where the home influence fails to support the teachers' values, the anti-academic culture is given free rein. This study is not competent to assess the relative power of such influences, but we cannot afford to ignore them.

A basic question concerns the amount of time that boys spend

in various forms of recreational activity outside school. A simple
index is the amount of time boys spend at home each evening.
Each boy was thus asked to estimate the average number of
evenings a week when he remained at home. If the boy did not
leave his home after six o'clock, this counted as an evening at
home. The results are given in Table XXXV, where we can see

TABLE XXXV

Evenings at Home

Form	Mean Evenings at home	N
4A	3·17	30
4B	1·64	28
4C	1·74	23
4D	1·95	22
All	2·18	103

that members of the A stream stay at home during the evening
more often than members of the other three streams, which are
almost equivalent in spending between one and a half and two
evenings at home. Boys in 4A and 4B were given homework.

4A spent an average of 46 minutes per evening in this way,
4B an average of 36 minutes. Although homework was frequently
saved up over several days and then completed in one evening,
the existence of homework may in part account for the tendency
of A stream boys to stay at home more. Within 4A boys in the
upper half of the informal status rankings tend to remain at
home slightly *less* than the lower half and spend slightly *more*
time on homework.

Yet the difference in the number of evenings spent at home
between 4A and the other three streams cannot be accounted
for simply in terms of homework. For example, we would expect
to find that the boys who stay at home more tend to watch
television more. This is confirmed by Table XXVI, though the

TABLE XXXVI

Television Viewing

Form	Mean hours per day		N
	Monday to Thursday	*Friday to Sunday*	
4A	3·32	4·72	30
4B	2·80	4·52	28
4C	3·17	4·61	23
4D	3·00	4·30	23
All	3·08	4·55	104

differences between streams are slight. Thus the tendency for A stream boys to spend more time at home in the evening is associated with their tendency to spend more time on homework and watch more television.[6]

What other factors could cause the 4A boys to spend more

TABLE XXXVII

Reading Habits

Form	% *Active members of Public Library*	*Mean books read during past month*	% *Having read no books in past month*	N
4A	50	2·4	33	30
4B	7	1·1	33	28
4C	0	0·9	59	23
4D	4	1·5	52	22
All	17	1·5	43	103

evenings at home? Do they, for example, read more? Table XXXVII shows that such may be the case; they are more often members of the Public Library and they read more books on average than other streams. We may note that virtually none of the lower stream boys are members of the Public Library and over half had not read a book in the past month.

Table XXXVIII gives the club affiliations of the fourth year boys. A distinction has been made between different kinds of club. 73 per cent of A stream boys attend *organized* clubs regularly and this proportion declines steadily to 30 per cent in the D stream. The results thus indicate that the higher the stream, the greater the tendency for boys to join clubs which are specially designed and organized for young people. When we consider the *un-*

TABLE XXXVIII

Club Affiliation

Club	% *Attending weekly*			
	4A	4B	4C	4D
Boys' Club	50	25	26	4
Scouts	7	—	—	—
Boys' Brigade	3	7	9	13
British Legion	10	—	—	—
Church Youth Club	10	4	9	4
Service Cadets	3	—	4	—
At least one organized club*	73	39	43	30
Billiard Hall	20	29	35	48
'Beat' Club	3	11	26	35
At least one unorganized club*	20	39	43	52

*Chi-square = 9·99   D.f. = 3   P<0·25

organized clubs, the reverse trend appears: the lower the stream the greater the tendency to join such clubs.

The organized clubs listed in the Table require no description. Of the unorganized clubs, the billiard hall ('pill-hall') was the more popular. This was housed in a prefabricated building on the fringe of the school's catchment area. Some eight billiard tables were available plus a small bar which offered light refreshments. It was, of course, mainly patronized by local male residents and had its own team. During the day the club was less busy than in the evenings, but during the afternoons it accommodated the retired, the shift-workers and the unemployed. During the lunch hour and sometimes immediately after afternoon school, members of the C and D streams, especially the delinquent group boys, would visit the club and when they were able to afford it, play a game of snooker. The manager seemed happy to allow these boys into the club since they did bring some custom and were potential patrons. However, after some trouble the manager barred a number of Lumley boys from the premises and he told me that he intended to raise the minimum age for membership to sixteen years. Six months later this threat to the boys had not been carried out. One or two of the boys were promising players and received some encouragement from the adult players, but in general they were ignored. The delinquent group members used to sit quietly, smoking and watching the games.

The 'beat' club, which was also situated at the edge of the school's catchment area, was a club designed specially for persons under the age of 21 years. Its membership consisted in the main of adolescents of the 13–17 range. This club had no organized activities and no subscription. There was dancing to records and to 'groups'. Members were able to buy light refreshments. Male members were in the majority and the club had a reputation for its 'roughness': fights were a fairly frequent occurrence. Most of the A and B stream boys thought it to be 'unrespectable', 'scruffy' and 'rough'.

We may note that the delinquent group frequented the billiard hall and the beat club more often than either the upper streams or the rest of the two lower streams, but the reasons for this will be discussed later. For the moment, let it suffice to point out that the upper streams, and especially 4A, contained boys who tended to belong to clubs which are non-profitmaking, educational and organized purposefully for young people. The members of the lower streams, and some proportion of 4B, preferred to attend either the billiard hall with its predominantly adult membership and ethos, or the beat club which was profit-making, non-educational and more autonomous. The trend of lower stream pupils is thus to reject supervision of leisure activities.

Boys in lower streams raised three objections to the Boys' club which was attended by half the A stream, but only 4 per cent of 4D. Firstly, it was 'boring' in its stress on competitive games like table tennis and its concern with physical education and the leaders' attempts to organize them. Secondly, they objected to the small size of the billiard tables. Since snooker was their favourite game, the full-sized tables and the lack of supervision made the billiard hall a much more attractive proposition. Thirdly, the Boys' Club required a weekly subscription. If a boy did not attend the Club for several weeks, he was still forced to pay subscriptions for the intervening period. In this way the club demanded very regular attendance, which due to the other factors mentioned above, low stream boys were unprepared to give.

Whereas the low stream boys restricted their leisure pursuits almost exclusively to the Lumley area, boys in 4A tended to be

TABLE XXXIX

Cinema Attendance

Form	% *More than once a week*	% *Once a week*	% *Once a month*	% *Occasionally*	% *Rarely or never*	*N*
4A	—	13	13	13	60	30
4B	7	25	4	7	57	28
4C	30	30	4	4	30	23
4D	26	35	4	—	35	23
All	14	25	7	7	47	104

If the first three and the last two columns are combined to form a two-column matrix, then

Chi-square $= 12.61$ D.f. $= 3$ $P < .01$

much more adventurous. Adrian and Arnold, for example, were very keen on climbing and pot-holing. Adrian joined a Club which organized climbing expeditions and sponsored lectures on relevant matters. During the year a number of other high status boys in 4A developed similar interests. Visits by cycle to local places of interest and fishing trips were by no means uncommon. During the year 4A held competitions in chess and draughts. A number of boys possessed fine stamp collections. All these things were very rare in low stream boys; as we saw in Chapter Three, they tended not to approve of boys who had interesting hobbies.

Low stream boys tend to visit the cinema much more frequently than high stream boys (see Table XXXIX).[9] Some sixty per cent of C and D stream boys go at least once a week. This fact illustrates again the tendency for low stream boys to seek out passive and independent activities in their leisure time pursuits.

A few of the upper stream boys attended some of the dance halls and more 'respectable' beat clubs, but only spasmodically. Lower stream boys confined themselves to the one 'beat club', but according to their accounts few of them actually danced.

There is no major difference between streams in extent of church attendance, as indicated in Table XL. It can be seen that 15 per cent of the boys attend at least once a week. This figure, which may to some seem surprisingly high, may be artificially

TABLE XL

Church Attendance

Form	% More than once a week	% Once a week	% Once a month	% Occasionally	% Rarely or never	N
4A	13	7	20	33	27	30
4B	7	4	11	39	39	28
4C	4	4	26	30	35	23
4D	13	4	4	35	44	23
All	10	5	14	35	36	104

inflated by the tendency to over-estimate Church attendance noted by many investigators.

Leisure time activities might be a function of amount of available money. Table XLI shows that there are no differences in amount of pocket money between streams. These figures represent the total amount of spending money, whether given by parents or earned from a part-time job or a combination of both. Table XLII shows that there is some evidence that boys from higher streams are more likely to secure part-time employment.[10]

TABLE XLI

Weekly pocket money

Form	Average (shillings)
4A	14·60
4B	15·02
4C	13·95
4D	14·09
All	14·41

TABLE XLII

Part-time job

Form	% With job
4A	37
4B	54
4C	26
4D	26
All	37

Table XLIII shows that 86 per cent of Lumley fourth year boys *supported* a professional football or rugby team. Support is here defined as following the career of a particular team through the season. Thus 14 per cent have no interest in such sports. 23 per cent never attend a game; the majority attend occasionally. There is no significant difference between streams.

Ninety per cent of the fourth year boys at Lumley had definite 'pop' group preferences (see Table XLIV). Each boy was given two choices and twenty such groups were mentioned. These were divided into two categories. The first, referred to as the 'long-haired groups', contains those groups who not only have long hair but which most adults consider to be 'rough' or 'scruffy'. Both adults and pupils agreed that this category, which

TABLE XLIII

Professional Football and Rugby

Form	Supporting a team %	ATTENDANCE					N
		More than week	Once a week	Once a month	Occasion-ally	Never	
4A	77	17	3	13	33	33	30
4B	92	21	12	—	48	18	27
4C	86	9	23	14	41	14	22
4D	90	14	9	24	29	24	21
All	86	16	11	12	38	23	100

included the Rolling Stones, the Kinks, Them and the Pretty Things, could be distinguished from other groups. Nearly two thirds of the boys preferred the long-haired groups to others, but this trend is less marked in the A stream. Of special note is the fact that the delinquent group chooses the long-haired variety almost to the exclusion of other groups, whereas the remaining members of the C and D stream split their votes between the two types.

TABLE XLIV

'Pop' Group Choices

Groups	*4A*	*4B*	*4C*	*4D*	*D-Group*	*Rest*	*All Forms*
'Long-haired' groups	53	69	68	61	87	40	62
Other groups	35	26	30	16	7	40	27
No choice	12	6	2	23	7	19	10

We may summarize the section in the generalization that the higher the stream, the more time boys spend at home, the more time they spend on homework, the more they read, the more they belong to organized clubs and less to unorganized clubs, the more they watch television, the less they go to the cinema, and the less they prefer long-haired 'pop' groups.

Chapter Eight

TWO SUBCULTURES

The various chapters of this study combine to give us a (somewhat disjointed) picture of the differentiation of the values and behaviour of boys in different streams at Lumley Secondary Modern School. The boys are not distributed throughout the streams in a random way; rather, from our knowledge of a particular boy's stream we can within limits predict some of the main values he will tend to hold. We have seen that the higher the stream of a boy, the greater the tendency for him to be committed to the school's values. His attendance at school is more regular and his participation in school activities is deeper. He likes school and the teachers, to whose expectations he conforms, whose values he supports and whose approval he seeks. This trend is particularly true of 4A boys, and as we move from the highest stream to the lowest, this trend tends to reverse itself, and the values held by low stream pupils are the opposite of those held by their peers in 4A.

Our examination of the normative structure of each form revealed a clear variation in the criteria on which boys assess one another and derive status or prestige in the informal group in different streams. We find that in the A stream informal status correlates positively with academic achievement and behaviour rating scores, whereas in the low streams informal status is a function of a negative orientation to the school's values. The A stream boys approve of the teacher's conception of his own role and define the pupil role in terms of conformity to the teacher expectations. In the low streams, the boys do not approve of the teacher's definition of his own role and disapprove of pupils who meet the teachers' definition of the pupil role.

This process of differentiation reveals itself, as we saw at the beginning, in the friendship choices made among the fourth year pupils (Table I). In each form the majority of boys choose their friends from their own form. This is hardly surprising, since it is with his class-mates that each individual interacts most frequently during school hours, and often outside school as well. But we must also note that although between a quarter and a third of friends are chosen from other streams, these extra-form choices are not random. The process of selection of friends from other streams can be summarized in the generalization that the greater the distance between streams, the lower the proportion of friendship ties.

In two cases, 4B and 4C, the form has two adjacent streams, one higher and one lower. Inspection of the table shows that boys in 4B choose friends from 4A more often than they do from 4C; and boys in 4C choose friends from 4D more often than they do from 4B. Why should this be so? Several possible explanations suggest themselves. It may be a result of the school's policy of transferring boys from one stream to another on the basis of terminal examination results. This fact allows two possible explanations. The first is that if boys transferred *to* 4B originate more often from the A rather than the C stream, then these boys might tend to prefer boys from 4A rather than from 4C, since they are choosing boys with whom they formerly interacted more frequently. Table XLV shows this to be so: 38 per cent of 4B boys come from the A stream originally, whereas only 14 per cent came from the C stream. But this explanation does not hold for 4C's extra-form friendship choice tendency. 41 per cent of 4C were transferred from the B stream, and only 9 per cent from the D stream, which is the reverse of the prediction. The second possible explanation in terms of the transfer system is that if boys are transferred *from* the B stream to the A stream more often than to the C stream, then the boys who remain in the B stream are more likely to choose A boys than C boys as friends, since they will be choosing boys with whom they formerly had great opportunity for interaction. This is true for the C stream, where 26 per cent of C stream boys were transferred to the D stream, but only 14 per cent to the B stream. But it does not hold for 4B, since 41 per cent of the B stream boys were transferred to the C stream and 31 per cent to the A stream. The results of the friendship choice distribution cannot be explained by either of these two possibilities, unless they are combined.

It could be argued that these explanations are inadequate since they take no account of the *recency* of the transfers. Let us consider the transfers that took place at the end of the third year. If the differential choice process is the result of these transfers, then the newcomers, that is, those who have been transferred, should account for the tendency more than the core members, that is, those who have not been transferred. The relevant figures are given in Table XLVI. Whilst it is true that newcomers in 3B choose their friends from adjacent streams more often than do core members, they do not prefer A boys to C boys more often than core members. In 4C, we find that the newcomers choose 4D boys *less* often than core members. This explanation, then, does not account for the facts.

TABLE XLV

Fourth Year Forms by Forms of Origin

Fourth Year Form	FORM OF ORIGIN					N
	A	*B*	*C*	*D*	*E*	
4A	48	31	14	3	3	29
4B	38	48	14	—	—	29
4C	14	41	36	9	—	22
4D	—	9	26	39	26	23
4E	—	6	6	13	75	16

Figures are percentages.

Although the above factors may play some part, we shall argue that the differential distribution of choices in the two central streams can be most adequately interpreted as an expression of a cultural dichotomy between the upper (A and B) streams and the lower (C and D) streams. In short, we are suggesting that the fourth year can be divided into two 'subcultures'. The upper stream subculture, embodied in the leadership of Adrian, is characterized by values which are positively orientated to the

TABLE XLVI

Analysis of Choices to Adjacent Forms

Choice Donors	% of Choices given to:		
4B	4A	4B	4C
All 4B	11	77	6
Newcomers	20	56	15
Core Members	9	84	4
4C	4B	4C	4D
All 4C	7	70	17
Newcomers	18	63	9
Core Members	3	72	20

school and the teachers. The lower stream subculture, embodied in the leadership of Clint, is characterized by values which are negatively orientated to the school. The lower streams take the upper stream values and 'turn them upside down' and thus form an example of what Cohen terms a *negative polarity*.[1] The differentiation of values, though a continuum, is focused in two opposite poles of attraction which produce a gap in the friendship choices between the B and C streams.

We shall term these two suggested subcultures 'academic' and 'delinquescent'. 'Academic' indicates that the values are orientated to those of the school and the teachers; 'delinquescent' indicates that the values are negatively orientated towards school, and in the direction of delinquent values, though not of course being synonymous with delinquency. To posit the existence of such subcultures is to propose a model or 'ideal type' of the school's cultural structure. To what extent such an analysis 'fits' Lumley Secondary Modern School, that is to what extent it can serve as a meaningful and useful interpretative summary of our findings, has still to be justified. The 'ideal type' is presented pictorially in Diagram I. The dominant values of the A and B streams are academic, though this is less true for the B stream; delinquescent values in these forms are deviant. In the C and D streams, the dominant values are delinquescent, though this is less true for the C stream, and academic values are deviant. Thus the A and D streams become the poles or extremes of the normative differentiation.

Representation of Two Subcultures

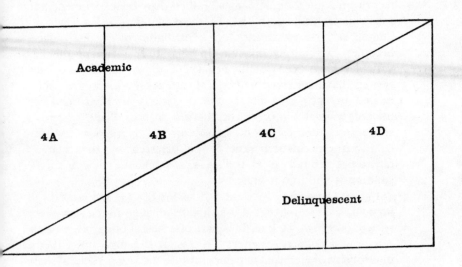

DIAGRAM I.

Subcultural differentiation is a *process* which takes place over time, and if our analysis is to be valid, we must be able to elucidate its development from the first to the fourth years at Lumley. That much of the evidence presented in previous chapters makes sense in terms of this model is obvious, but a study of the fourth year alone gives us little information with which to explain its origin. We shall shortly present some comparative material from second year boys, but first we must attempt to outline in a more general way some of the factors which influence this subcultural development. Much of what is to follow will be speculative, based on theoretical elaborations and an eclectic review of some current literature, but wherever possible the speculation will be rooted in evidence from Lumley School.

Most attempts at explanation in social science are beset by the multiplicity and inter-connections of the variables the researcher wishes to assess. Nor can one easily conduct experiments with human beings, although in recent years social scientists have devised many ingenious techniques for testing hypotheses about human behaviour. In studying the social process within a school, the researcher has to rely predominantly on observation and record and questionnaire data, rather than on experiments, to substantiate his hypotheses. The variables at work are almost infinite, and the assessment of the contribution of any one variable becomes exceedingly difficult. In this study many of the key variables have been totally neglected; those which have been treated have received superficial attention. They are inter-related in such a complex way, especially in their tendency towards mutual reinforcement, that the analysis of the process of subcultural differentiation soon leads to dangerous and un-confirmed speculation. Yet to be deterred by the inherent difficulties would be as foolish as to imagine that a simple solution is within our grasp.

Lumley Secondary Modern School for Boys is not a world of its own. We cannot regard it as independent from the rest of the society in which we live. It is part of a neighbourhood, a town, a region, a country, Western Europe. It is bound up with the multiplicity of elements which constitute the larger social system, and because of this much of what we have observed derives from, and must be analysed in terms of, the social system as a whole. The boys and teachers at Lumley are products as well as components of the social system.

We cannot enter into the complexities of sociological theory, but it is essential that we take note of sociological analyses of society. For our purposes, we must consider that Western Europe and America are stratified societies, which means that human beings are differentially ranked as superior or inferior relative to one another in certain respects. Society ranks its members in terms of social hierarchy. This is a complex process, since the criteria by which we rank persons are really a set of interrelated variables such as social origin, occupation, education, wealth, residence, power, speech and so on. But ours is not a caste system: the boundaries between social groupings are fluid rather than fixed. Yet we may conveniently distinguish between these social groupings or classes and examine the variation and similarity of values between classes.

Many, especially American, sociologists have been concerned to show that our society's values are based on what has been termed the Protestant ethic. That is, the key value of our society is *achievement*: man is saved by his individual works and strivings. We exist on the myth of equality of opportunity to achieve – the beggar may become a millionaire. We are thus subjected as members of this society to pressures towards striving to achieve. Sociologists are interested in the degree to which people are orientated towards this goal, and in the differences between social classes. Merton has suggested that the orientations of particular persons or groups towards these goals, combined with their perception of and access to the means by which these goals can be attained, can contribute to our understanding of the values of different persons and groups.[2]

The basic division made by sociologists between social classes distinguishes the non-manual from the manual workers, or the middle class from the working class. Moreover, they have sought to show that the values which dominate, namely those stemming from the Protestant ethic, with its stress on personal achievement, are basically those of the middle class. The working class may not be able to attain these goals, due to their restricted access to the means, but many of them accept the validity of the values, even though they may sometimes appear to reject them.

This brief excursus into some sociological writings is not extrinsic to our purpose, for we are now better equipped to place the school in its social framework. If one of the key values of our society is achievement, then the school becomes a central focus and means by which individuals can achieve. Its stress on academic achievement, which is a major determinant of future occupation, represents an embodiment of these societal values. In England the influence of academic achievement is revealed in the distinction between the Grammar Schools and the Secondary Modern Schools, for which children are selected on their 'success' in the competitive eleven-plus examination. That the nation has accurately perceived that entry to a Grammar School offers greater opportunity for academic and therefore social advancement and success is evidenced by the growing amount of parental concern over the child's results in the eleven-plus examination, and by the predominantly middle class opposition to the reorganization of secondary education on comprehensive lines. The fact that the eleven-plus examination is seen in terms of 'success' and 'failure' indicates that academic and social aspirations have undermined the somewhat unrealistic concern in England to provide a variety of secondary schools appropriate to the abilities and aptitudes of their pupils and that such schools should have, in the eyes of the public, 'parity of esteem'. The educational system selects and differentiates its pupils in a further manner, for the vast majority of secondary schools whether Grammar, Modern or Comprehensive, stream pupils by their achievement relative to one another. Though there may be good educational grounds for so doing – a question which cannot be answered here – we cannot ignore that the effect of streaming is to separate children with relatively greater academic achievement into 'higher' streams; and to most of the public 'higher' is synonymous with 'better'. To succeed at school is to succeed in society. To divide our children in this way means that we must also have children who 'fail', by not obtaining entry either to a Grammar school and/or to a high stream.

Concepts of 'success' or 'failure' in academic achievement thus form a reflection of societal values, which are most marked in the middle class, though sociologists maintain that such values are accepted as valid by many people of the working class, even when they do not adhere to them. The school is founded on, fosters and perpetuates those values which sociologists associate with the middle class, and the teachers themselves are mainly successful products of such schools, even though their social origin may be working class.

To what extent did the pupils at Lumley internalize and conform to middle class values, even though the school catchment area is working class? Cohen lists the middle class values as:

(i) Ambition is regarded as a virtue.

In our study we have seen that, the higher the stream the greater the parental support for desiring a better job than father's, and the higher the occupational aspirations of the boys.

(ii) Individual responsibility, resourcefulness and self-reliance.

No direct measures are available for these at Lumley, but we may note, for example, that high stream boys are more anxious than others to convince the teachers that they are able to work unsupervised, both in the class-room and at home, and they show greater interest in activities such as rock climbing and cycle tours.[3]

(iii) Cultivation and possession of skills.

In our study the higher the stream, the more the boys prefer to work hard at school, approve boys who do likewise, and like teachers who make the pupils work hard and punish boys who misbehave.

(iv) Worldly asceticism, postponing immediate satisfaction in the interest of long-term achievement.

This trend is most marked in the A stream at Lumley where boys value academic achievement more than 'having fun'. In the low streams the reverse is true. This difference reveals itself particularly in the norms which govern copying.

(v) Rationality and planning.

When the boys were asked to express their agreement or disagreement with the statement, 'Planning for the future is a waste of time', there was an association between disagreement and high stream (chi-square $= 8\cdot37$, D.f. $= 3$, $P < \cdot 05$).

(vi) Cultivation of manners, courtesy and personability.

Members of the low stream approve cheekiness to the teachers significantly more often than high stream boys, and a direct measure of approval of good manners differentiated between the streams.

(vii) Control of physical aggression and violence.

In the high streams, fighting ability is irrelevant to status, and fighting activity is deviant. In the low streams, physical powers and fighting ability form a major criterion of informal status.

(viii) Wholesome recreation.

High stream boys tend to join youth clubs which organize activities for their members, whereas low stream boys tend to join clubs which do not organize specific activities and in which members may play very passive roles. Approval of boys with 'interesting hobbies' is associated with high streams.

(ix) Respect for property.

Low stream boys, especially members of the delinquent group, are frequently involved in acts of theft and malicious damage, but this is not true for high stream boys.

In short, there is evidence in this study that the higher the stream the greater the degree of conformity to middle class values. Moreover, there were indications in the meagre evidence produced in Chapter Seven that high stream boys tend to come from homes which were more orientated to middle class values than were the homes of low stream boys.

At this point, the interrelationship of home and school variables becomes complex. That the values acquired in the home and the values held by the peer group reinforce each other seems a reasonable conclusion. The academic subculture thus predominantly consists of boys from homes which are more orientated to the middle class, and the pressures in the peer group are towards conformity to the middle class expectations of the teachers. In the delinquescent subculture, a majority of boys comes from homes which are less orientated to middle class values and the peer group exerts pressures towards non-conformity to the school's values. In cases at each extreme home and school are mutually reinforcing. When peer group and home influences are consistent, subcultural differentiation is considerably facilitated. When peer group and home conflict, the pupil is faced with a problem of adjustment.

We may consider the processes inherent in the school irrespective of home background. For boys in high streams life at school will be a pleasant and rewarding experience, since the school system confers status upon them. This status is derived from membership of a high stream, where boys are considered to be academically successful, and are granted privileges and responsibility in appointment as prefects and in their selection for school visits and holidays. The peer group values reflect the status bestowed on such boys by the school in being consonant with teachers' values. Conformity to peer group and school values is thus consistent and rewarding.

In the low streams, boys are deprived of status in that they are *double failures* by their lack of ability or motivation to obtain entry to a Grammar School or to a high stream in the Modern School. The school, as we have seen, accentuates this state of failure and deprivation. The boys have achieved virtually nothing. For boys in low streams, conformity to teacher expectations gives little status. We can thus regard the low stream boys as subject to status frustration, for not only are they unable to gain any sense of equality of worth in the eyes of the school, but their occupational aspirations for their future lives in society are seriously reduced in scope.[4]

The allocation and attitudes of teachers increase this divergence between the upper and lower streams. Whilst the fact that lower stream pupils are not entered for external examinations must inevitably lead to a reduction in motivation to achieve, the tendency to assign teachers with poorer qualifications and weaker discipline to these forms reduces even further the pressure exerted on such boys towards academic goals. Once teachers remove the incentive of examinations from these pupils, provide greater opportunities for indiscipline, and begin to expect little from them, it is hardly surprising that they become progressively retarded and alienated from the school's values.

Lumley school is selective in its educative process; there is a constant movement of boys between streams. Those with positive orientations towards the values of the school will tend over the four years to converge on the higher streams; and those with negative orientations will tend to converge on the low streams. On every occasion that a boys is 'promoted' or 'demoted' on the basis of school examinations, the greater becomes the concentration of the two opposing subcultures. As boys with similar values and attitudes are drawn together by this selective process, the more we would expect these values to persist and the greater will become the domination of subcultural values, leading to an increase in pressure towards conformity to the peer group. Demotion to the delinquescent subculture is unlikely to encourage a boy to strive towards academic goals, since the pressures within the peer group will confirm and reinforce the anti-academic attitudes which led to demotion, and the climate within the low streams will be far from conducive to academic striving. In order to obtain promotion from a low stream, a boy must deviate from the dominant anti-academic values and overcome the obstacle of pressures towards 'messing'.

This concentration of boys with similar orientations, which may well be a continuation of a process already established in the Primary School, not only increases the vulnerability of the individual to group pressures, but it also tends to insulate members of different streams from interaction and from mutual influence. Individuals become increasingly exposed to their own subculture and increasingly insulated from the values of the other. All these mutually reinforcing factors thus lead, by the fourth year, to a polarization of values.

At Lumley several aspects of the school organization, whilst intended purely as a convenience for the construction of the time-table, serve to reinforce this divergence between sub-cultures. If we examine the time-table we discover that all the boys in fourth year go to the games field on one particular morning of the week. The playing fields are several miles distant from the school, entailing a journey by bus. During the first two periods of the day members of 4A and 4B travel and play games together. After the mid-morning break, 4C and 4D do likewise. The same is true for Handicraft. The boys are asked to select woodwork or metalwork. Two thirds of the boys do woodwork in two workshops and the remaining third does metalwork. The boys are systematically rotated between woodwork and metal-work and between workshops. The significant point is that 4A and 4B take Handicraft simultaneously, as do 4C and 4D. Thus at any one stage we will find boys from *either* both the upper streams *or* both the lower streams taking Handicraft at the same time, but never upper and lower streams together.

The effect of this separation of the upper from the lower streams for Handicraft and Games is that they have differential opportunities for interaction. A boy of either the two upper or the two lower streams will, in these two subjects which enjoy six periods a week, be brought into immediate contact with the members of the other stream in his subculture, but not with members of the other subculture. In this way the structure of the time-table divides the streams into two halves and helps to account for the division in the friendship choices we observed at the beginning of the chapter, and for the normative differentiation, since this differential opportunity for interaction creates an artificial barrier to communication.

When we add to this the fact that members of upper streams have common teachers, common homework, and common school visits, we can see that these organizational elements may have far reaching effects on the pupils.

When we consider these differential opportunities for interaction and the convergence of boys with similar motives in upper and lower streams, it is hardly surprising that attitudes between streams should be so hostile, as we saw in Chapter Three. As Newcomb has pointed out,[5] barriers to communication are likely to lead to the formation of stereotypes, especially where a status-differential is involved; and as long as the barriers remain, the hostile attitudes will persist and perhaps be reinforced. By the fourth year the values and attitudes of members of upper and lower streams have diverged, and there is evidence of deep hostility between the A and the D streams. The barriers existing between the upper and lower halves reinforce the perceived differences and elevate them into irreconcilable and totally opposed stereotypes.

The teacher, whilst he is usually aware that anti-academic boys in high streams are deviant from the group norms, often fails to take adequate account of the fact that academically orientated boys in lower streams are also deviant from group norms. Deviance and conformity are defined in terms of the teacher's own definition of the pupil role, not in terms of peer group values. Because academic low stream boys conform to his expectations, he does not recognize their deviance from the group. To the teacher, it is the high status boys in the low streams who are deviant, yet it is in fact these very boys who are most integrated on a peer group level.

When the teacher rewards boys in high streams for good work or behaviour, he is confirming the dominant values amongst the boys. But when he does this to boys in lower streams, he is confirming the minority norms. In other words, teacher rewards demonstrate the *unification* of teacher and peer group values in high streams; but the same teacher rewards in low streams reveal the *disjunction* between teacher and pupil values. Teacher rewards thus confirm both subcultures, but in the lower streams this is the reverse of what the teacher intends, for by rewarding the deviant academically orientated boy he reinforces the dominant group values.[6] Teacher rewards cannot have their intended effect in low streams at Lumley until the boys as a whole accept the validity of his definition of teacher and pupil roles.

In the academic subculture, because the boys behave in conformity to teacher expectations, and because the two sets of values are consistent, the teacher is able to exert considerable control over the peer group. In the delinquescent subculture, the teachers have little power of social control, because of the conflict which exists between teacher and pupil values. Attempts to change the culture of low streams must thus begin with the conversion of the leaders or high status boys. When teachers regard the high status low stream boys as 'worthless louts' with whom they cannot afford to 'waste time', they are in fact discarding not only these few boys, but also their only means by which group change might be effected.

The members of the delinquescent subculture, if our contention that they are status-deprived is just, reject the system which confers this status and the values on which the status-system is based. Such boys are thus forced to seek a substitute system which can confer prestige in proportion to the degree of rejection of the school's values. It is through the anti-academic rejection of the school's values that informal status within the delinquescent group is achieved. They reject the pupil role and replace it with an autonomous and independent peer culture. Conformity thus becomes more important than in the academic subculture, where the boys are united through *individual* effort in academic competition. In the delinquescent subculture self-esteem is a *collective* product, since it can be obtained only in relation to the group as a whole, that is, through conformity to anti-academic group pressures, whereas in the academic subculture boys can develop self-esteem on the more individualistic basis of academic competence.

The members of the delinquescent subculture, then, seek alternatives to the pupil role as defined by the teachers. Their rejection of the pupil role is supported by the evidence in earlier chapters and need not be repeated here. The important point is that in re-defining the pupil role, such boys aspire to roles outside the terms of the school. Although the low stream pupil is legally forced to come to school, his status as a schoolboy is resented. One solution is to re-define the pupil role in terms of *adult* roles, as well as behaving in ways opposed to teacher definitions. The rejection of the pupil role and the associated status system leads to admiration and premature imitation of adult roles beyond the school. This aspiration towards adult roles is a measure of the rejection of the pupil role, for these boys anticipate their adult socialization before they take up the appropriate work-role outside the school. This premature and anticipatory adult socialization expresses itself in the exaggerated display of selected aspects of behaviour associated with adult status.[7] Members of the delinquescent subculture thus exhibit behaviour which symbolizes adult status, for example, smoking and drinking. The delinquent group smoked more cigarettes per day than any other group at Lumley and they frequently drank bottles of cheap wine or sherry in secret. To consume nicotine and alcohol, and to be seen to consume them, compensates for their lack of satisfaction in the pupil role.[8] One of the reasons why many members of the delinquescent subculture were so anxious to leave school was because they wanted to have their status at *home* changed from being a 'school boy' into a 'worker', for as workers they would be allowed to smoke openly at home and would no longer have to run errands for the family. As Derek replied when I asked him what would be the nicest thing about starting work :

Walking in the house at night with a fag in my gob.

We need no longer wonder why the billiard hall was such an attraction to low stream boys.

The implication of much of this analysis is that there is a real sense in which the school can be regarded as a generating factor of delinquency.[9] Although the aims and efforts of the teachers are directed towards deleting such tendencies, the organization of the school and its influence on subcultural development unintentionally foster delinquent values. The influence of the school on the delinquent group cannot be discussed unless we have a framework in which to set our ideas. Albert Cohen, to whose ideas the present writer is indebted, has suggested a theory to account for the existence of delinquency as almost entirely a working class, male phenomenon.[10] His argument, which cannot be adequately treated here, states that the working class boy is handicapped in his achievement in the middle class system and that this differential access to the means for this achievement produces a status-frustration, especially since the working class boy is constantly surrounded by middle class agents who emphasize his lack of status. Such boys are thus faced with a problem of adjustment to which delinquency is one of several possible solutions.

Miller, however, believes that gang delinquency is primarily generated through a lower class culture;[11] that is to say, working class boys can learn certain values and behaviour patterns which are already normative within the working class culture, with its 'focal concerns' of law violation, physical prowess, freedom from restraint, shrewdness, desire for 'thrills' and concept of fate. For Miller, delinquency is a form of integration into working class culture, whereas for Cohen the delinquent cannot be really integrated into working class culture because he is frustrated by his inability to succeed in terms of the 'middle class measuring rod'. If Cohen's argument is to stand, it needs to show that the working class delinquent is indeed surrounded by middle class agents by which his lack of status may be induced. Such boys are indeed exposed to middle class values through the mass media, especially television; but their main exposure will be through the school, where they spend a considerable proportion of their youth and where they are subjected to the middle class values of the teachers. The teacher thus becomes the principal *direct* agent by which the working class boy is exposed to middle class values. High stream boys can internalize and abide by such values, since it is in the acquisition of such values that their hopes of future success are contained. For low stream boys, however, the school simultaneously exposes them to these values and deprives them of status in these terms.[12] It is at this point that they may begin to reject the values because they cannot succeed in them. More than this, the school provides a mechanism through the streaming system whereby their failure is effected and institutionalized, and also provides a situation in which they can congregate together in low streams.

It is at this point that a group solution becomes both more urgent and more possible. As Cohen points out:

. . . it is a hallmark of subcultural delinquency that it is acquired and practised in groups rather than independently contrived by the individual as a solution to his private problems.[13]

In other words, the crucial condition for the emergence of the subculture is the existence of a *group* of persons with the same problem of adjustment, and Cohen points out the paucity of research which has investigated the factors influencing the creation and selection of solutions. It is our contention that the school is an influence both in the determination of the status deprivation and in the creation of conditions in which the subculture can form and define itself.[14]

Cohen goes on to suggest some of the mechanisms by which a group solution can occur, especially in his discussion of 'exploratory gestures'. By this he means that persons with the same problem of adjustment, which cannot be solved legitimately in terms of the dominant culture, will initiate solutions in a tentative way by probing gestures of mutual exploration. By a process of joint acceptance and elaboration of the exploratory gestures a solution is arrived at. Those elements which are most rewarding to the group and which most facilitate a solution form the basis of group culture. This study cannot, of course, offer a systematic body of evidence to substantiate this hypothesis, but some of the material, such as the early history of Clint and Clem, is by no means inconsistent with the theory.

Before we continue, let us summarize our theoretical, 'ideal type' analysis. We suggest that subcultural development is a function of a number of mutually reinforcing variables. The first of these is the home, which predisposes the child to an acceptance or rejection of the school values and which affects the child's career in school and the way in which he will be integrated into or isolated from his peer group values. The second important factor is the organization of the School. At Lumley, the structure of the time-table led to differential opportunities for interaction for boys in upper and lower streams and the consequent segregation favoured the development of common values within each half and of negative stereotypes between halves. This factor also includes the allocation of teachers. The system of transfers between streams leads to a convergence of boys with similar orientations in the same stream. Thirdly, the pressures towards conformity to the informal norms of the stream increase the pressures towards uniformity of values, even when these are inconsistent with those of teachers or parents. The fourth factor concerns the tendency of teachers to favour and reward high stream boys at the expense of their peers in low streams.

All these factors mutually reinforce one another – what engineers call 'positive feedback'. When the school system is viewed in the setting of societal values, the upper stream members are 'successful' and their efforts and values are rewarded by the status they derive. The low stream boys are 'failures'; they are status deprived both in the school and in society; their efforts meet with little success. Their problem of adjustment is solved by a rejection of societal and teacher values, which are substituted with a set of peer group values, and status is derived from conformity to a reversal of societal and teacher values.

To show that this is indeed a process which occurs over time now becomes essential to our analysis of subcultural differentiation and of the influence of the school in generating delinquency. The difficulty is that intensive study of fourth year boys at Lumley tells us very little about the influence of the previous three years in the school. Ideally, we would like to have the same measures on the same group of boys over a period of four years; on this basis we could assess the changes that had taken place during the time interval. In this study we have made mere speculation about the process, based on inferences from evidence about fourth year boys. There is no adequate way in which our analysis can be verified in the terms of this study, but we can offer some comparative material on *second* year boys which may be regarded as slight evidence for the suggested analysis. (We have, of course, to remember that we are now comparing two groups of different boys at different stages of their school careers, which is a method considerably inferior to one in which the same group of boys is tested at different stages.) From these second year pupils, who were also streamed into five forms, three sorts of evidence have been collected, for which three hypotheses can be erected.

Firstly, the Sentence Completion Test was administered to them. If our analysis of the process of normative and subcultural differentiation is correct we should expect that these items should fail to differentiate between streams, or differentiate between them at a much lower level of statistical significance.

Secondly, these pupils completed seven selected items from the multiple choice Orientation Test. The prediction is similar to that for the Sentence Completion Test.

Thirdly, behavioural ratings by teachers on each boy were collected and correlations between informal status and behaviour, and between informal status and academic position, were calculated. Three predictions follow from this.

(a) It should be untrue, or less true than in the fourth year, that the higher the stream, the higher the average behavioural score.

(b) The correlations between informal status and academic position should be similar for all streams, and should be positive rather than negative.

(c) The correlations between informal status and behavioural scores should be similar for all streams, and should be positive rather than negative.

The results are given in Tables XLVII and XLVIII. On the Sentence Completion Test, three out of the six items which differentiate between fourth year streams also differentiate between second year streams. Since three out of the six items do not differentiate between second year forms, and one differentiates at a lower level of significance than for the fourth year, there is some evidence for the prediction. In the results to the items of Orientation Test, only one of the seven items differentiates between second year streams at a statistically significant level. We can thus regard the prediction as verified.[15]

The average behaviour scores for each second year stream do in fact cluster together, the largest differences between forms being 0·16 whereas the fourth year figure is 0·68. Moreover, the average scores do not decline as we descend the streams; 2D has the highest average. We may thus conclude that behavioural scores are not stream-related in the second year, though they are in the fourth year (see Table XI). None of the correlations between informal status and academic position in second year forms reaches significance level; they are all close to nought. Moreover, the decline from positive to negative correlations with stream which was found for the fourth year forms does not hold in the second year. The correlations between informal status and behaviour are all negative in the second year and do not follow the progression from significantly positive in the A

stream to significantly negative in the D stream which we found
for fourth year boys. This finding is in line with the prediction

TABLE XLVII

Comparison Between Second and Fourth Year Streams (A)

Dimensions	Second Year		Fourth Year	
	Chi-square	P-value	Chi-square	P-value
Boys in the A stream are . . .	15·44	<·005	17·17	<·001
Boys in the D stream are . . .	31·39	<·001	13·51	<·005
Teachers are . . .	4·51	Not sig.	14·48	<·005
Teachers think of me as . . .	2·56	Not sig.	16·50	<·001
When lessons are boring I . . .	7·41	Not sig.	9·62	<·025
When teacher says my work is bad . . .	10·69	<·025	7·82	<·05
Teachers who control the class	8·39	<·05	8·43	<·05
Teachers who make boys work	5·08	Not sig.	18·69	<·001
Boy who pays attention	2·56	Not sig.	19·16	<·001
Boy who obeys	2·01	Not sig.	14·45	<·005
Boy who works hard	2·24	Not sig.	23·16	<·001
Boy who lets you copy	3·80	Not sig.	13·05	<·005
Boy you have fun with in lessons	0·85	Not sig.	8·94	<·05

For each chi-square test, 3 degrees of freedom.

TABLE XLVIII

Comparisons Between Second and Fourth Year Streams (B)

DIMENSION	YEAR	A Stream	B Stream	C Stream	D Stream
Informal Status and Academic Position	Second	+·10	−·06	+·16	−·17
	Fourth	+·50*	+·16	−·15	−·15
Informal Status and Behaviour	Second	−·37*	−·52*	−·13	−·37*
	Fourth	+·50*	−·12	−·58*	−·57*
Form Average Behaviour Score	Second	3·44	3·33	3·35	3·49
	Fourth	3·92	3·57	3·56	3·24

*Statistically significant.

in that the correlations tend to be similar, but it is difficult to explain why three of them should be significantly negative. (An *ad hoc* hypothesis might be that in the second year, when pressures towards academic achievement are not strong, it is the boys who tend to misbehave who acquire high status in all streams; after the second year, when academic pressures are exerted on high streams, criteria of status change in high and especially the A streams, but continue in the same direction in low streams.)[15]

We may conclude that there is no evidence of normative or subcultural differentiation between streams in the second year.[16] This supports our contention that this differentiation is a process which takes place during the four years at school, and also confirms the claims of the teachers that the low streams become 'difficult' only in the third and fourth years. It may of course be that either or both the second and fourth years are atypical; certainly it would be preferable if we had evidence on one year group tested in the second and fourth years. Our conclusion about the process of normative and subcultural differentiation must be regarded as tentative and subject to more detailed testing – but there is no evidence in this study *against* the analysis.

If it is true that normative differentiation and subcultural development do not become marked until the third and fourth years, then it is possible that status deprivation does not constitute, or is not perceived as, a problem for the younger boys. This is consistent with our analysis in that the mutual reinforcement of the key factors we have suggested will take time to be effective. Moreover, the perception of status deprivation in low stream boys will be in part a function of their realization of their societal as well as their scholastic failure. That is, the relation between stream and external examinations, and between academic success and the occupational structure, does not become a reality until the later years of life at school.

The subcultures persist year after year because the school system persists unchanged and unchallenged. The same problems produce the same solutions, especially when we consider the function of senior boys in providing role-models for younger boys.[17] Thus younger, low stream boys learn that fighting ability and delinquescent orientations are the bases of informal status to their elders. The subcultures are perpetuated over the years.

It is now time to put our feet back on the ground; speculation is a seductive and dangerous path. Our distinction between the academic and the delinquescent subcultures is a considerable over-simplification of the facts. Although the extremes can be clearly distinguished, there remains a large proportion of boys who, whilst tending towards one of the poles, cannot easily be contained in either. This is particularly true of 4B boys, who are often closer to the D stream's orientation than to the A stream's, as an examination of some of the Tables will confirm. 4B is an intermediate form in conflict between the two poles. It may be true that in other years the B stream will be drawn more towards A stream values, especially when we remember that in the fourth year considered here the most academically orientated members of the B stream were assigned to the A stream for C.S.E. purposes and replaced by the least academically orientated members of the A stream, a fact which has led to a somewhat artificial increase in the difference between the two. This may well have produced a dominance of non-academic values as we observed in Chapter Two, where we pointed out that 4B members tended to perceive themselves as 'leavers', by which the morale and prestige of the

B stream was lowered from its traditional near-equality with the A stream.

Perhaps our major unsolved problem is to explain the existence of deviants in each subculture. Why do boys persist in non-conformity to peer group norms? It is possible that for deviants in either subculture home background plays a powerful role. For example, low status low stream boys deviate from the peer group because they are sufficiently gratified by the teacher rewards they derive from hard work and acceptance of school values to be able to reject peer group pressures. Values internalized in the home may provide a reservoir of resistance against informal norms, so that they continue to resist even when they are unable, through lack of ability, to ascend into the higher streams to which they aspire. Why these low status low stream boys deviate in the face of powerful pressures from the dominant group is a fundamental question; they either have a different problem of adjustment or they find a different solution. In this study we have insufficient knowledge of the effect of our variables on *individuals* to be able to proffer an answer. This is particularly true of the deviants in the academic subculture, who make such an interesting compromise between the two poles. It is at this point that other variables, such as personality, which have been excluded from this study, may play such a critical part.

It may be that our analysis of the subcultural differentiation raises more problems than it solves. Certainly it has been speculative; and it is based on empirical data from one single school. Both these facts are serious weaknesses, and underline the dangers of making generalizations from this study. It is possible that the structure of social relations in Lumley Secondary Modern School for Boys is typical of many similar schools in Britain. Only when we treat this analysis of Lumley as a set of hypotheses for testing on a wider basis will the generality of our conclusions be known.

Chapter Nine

SOME IMPLICATIONS

Lumley Secondary Modern School for Boys is not, I believe, a very exceptional school. At the same time there are many schools in this country with greater problems and fewer resources; and there are many more schools where the problems are less intense and the resources are more adequately deployed in the exercise of more positive educational functions. To make generalizations from this research about secondary schools in general would be both pretentious and dangerous. For this reason our discussion of the implications of this study must be confined to Lumley School itself. Yet I hope that some of the implications drawn from this research will be relevant to other schools with common problems. In particular, this study may provide useful suggestions for other schools in 'problem areas'.

The first eight chapters of this book consist largely of a descriptive analysis, with supportive statistical evidence, of the structure of social relations in one school. I have tried to confine myself to this 'objective' task and to exclude value judgements on the school organization or on individual persons. Much of the analysis has been concerned with the unintended consequences of organization and human action within the school, and the deleterious effect of many of these on the educative process has been heavily implied. It is now time to make some of these implied value judgements explicit.

Perhaps the main consequence of this study has been to affirm the fundamental importance of the social system of the school, and especially the structure of peer groups, in relation to the educative process. One of the tasks of future educational research will be to investigate the ways in which home and other external influences interact with those internal to the school. Yet it is these in-school forces which have been neglected by teachers and researchers alike. The teachers at Lumley constantly under-estimated or were ignorant of the power of the peer group in regulating the behaviour of pupils. It was common practice for the teachers to shed the blame for many difficulties which might be caused or reinforced by the school itself on to the home environment. Yet the belief that children are 'difficult' in school *because* they come from 'difficult' homes is a convenient over-simplification. At Lumley, the misbehaviour of low stream boys was often 'explained' by the teachers in terms of a popular psychology or sociology. A teacher once remarked to me, 'Well, what can you expect? That lad's got no father' – but he failed to appreciate that the most hard-working member of the 'intel-lectual' B clique in 4A was also fatherless.

Once in school children become part of a social system and are subjected to a variety of influences. Most important of all, they become members of a group of age-mates, most often from the same stream. These groups have values, norms and status hierarchies which every member must take into account. These pressures towards conformity to the peer group will be especially powerful after the third year in secondary school with the onset of the 'adolescent syndrome'.[1] We know from many other studies that the mid-teens is a period when many young people begin to reject the authority of parents and teachers; when they begin to emancipate themselves from adults in their desire to liberate themselves from childhood dependency. The adolescent is in transition from childhood to adulthood; being no longer a child but not yet an adult, he has no valid autonomous status in the eyes of his elders. It is at this point that young people tend to fall back on the peer group, for it is with their age-mates that they most interact and from whom independent status may be derived. Moreover, adolescence is a period in which the search for a self-identity is most marked, and in which many basic social attitudes are acquired. Personality is not a static but a dynamic and changing process to which peer group membership may make a fundamental contribution.

It is within this general framework that subcultural differentia-tion takes place. For boys in low streams the onset of the adoles-cent syndrome is concomitant with the perception of status deprivation within school and its extension into their future careers. The association between low stream and delinquency at

Lumley may be as much the result of school and peer group influence on personality development as of the fact that the school tends to select certain personality types into different streams.

A central aim of education is to organize the school in such a way that *all* the pupils are educated to the full extent of their potentialities. An equally important educational goal is the integration of the pupils into the social life of the school. That is, the school should provide opportunities for, and stimulate motives conducive to, the development of satisfying and co-operative relationships between pupils and teachers and between pupils in different streams. Neither of these goals was achieved at Lumley School. The boys in the lower streams seem to have become progressively retarded by the fourth year, and their relationships with both teachers and high stream boys were hostile. It is tragic that often an A stream boy was not on speaking terms with a D stream boy, even though both may have been pupils in the same class in Junior School and both may live in the same street.

If the academic and social goals of education are to be achieved whilst retaining the streaming system, it is essential that the formation of two opposed subcultures is prevented at Lumley. This means, in effect, that the school must take steps to eradicate the status deprivation of low stream boys. At this school, as in many others, the low streams are not 'difficult' in the first two years, but only from the third year onwards. The foundations of the child's experience of school in his later years are laid during the first two. Attempts to solve the problem of the 'difficult' low stream boys only when they appear in the third year cannot hope to succeed. The seeds of status deprivation are sown at an earlier stage.

As long as boys are streamed by ability/attainment, and as long as only upper stream boys are entered for external examination, members of low streams will tend to feel deprived. To avoid this situation would require the complete abolition of our selective examination system. But let us confine our remarks to reforms which are feasible at Lumley School. Here the children are in fact divided into sheep and goats: those who take the examinations and those who do not. Those who are not allowed to take the external examinations will perceive, quite accurately, that their occupational aspirations must be relatively lower, since many skilled occupations are closed to those without formal educational qualifications. At Lumley the Local Leaving Certificate – which is now being replaced by the Certificate in Secondary Education – gave most of the A and B stream boys a written qualification with which to approach their future employers, but very few of the C and none of the D stream boys were allowed to enter for the examination. Don of 4D wished to enter for the examination because he wished to obtain an apprenticeship after leaving school. Although his form teacher approached the Headmaster about this, permission for Don to enter was refused. There is little doubt that the Headmaster and some of the teachers were anxious to be as near as possible to the top of the 'league table' of local schools taking this examination by maintaining a high proportion of successful entrants. Yet this percentage of passes is in part a function of the number of entries. Lumley could not achieve a high rank in the 'league table' unless boys whose chances of success in the examination were small were excluded from entry. In this way the school could maintain an apparently good academic record by depriving low stream pupils of the opportunity to enter for an external examination. (The 'league table' should preferably be abolished. If it is retained, a more accurate assessment of a school's academic record would be obtained if the 'league table' were constructed on the basis of the number of passes as a proportion of the whole fourth year population of the school rather than of the number of entries.)

The influence of external examinations goes further than this. If the low stream pupils are not entered for the examination, then the diluted form of the examination course which often forms the basis of their curriculum may be inappropriate. Certainly we cannot expect such boys to be motivated to work hard academically. If the examination is the carrot by which we entice the horse to run, we should not be surprised if the horse stands still when we take the carrot away. One of the principal reasons for the progressive retardation and the development of a delinquescent subculture among the low streams is the fact that they are unlikely to be motivated to work hard at school because they cannot see any useful or tangible reward for their labours.

A similar process is at work among the teachers. We have already noted the differential allocation of teachers to the various streams and need not repeat it here. The point is that none of the teachers feels under the same pressure to motivate or stimulate the low stream pupils because the lack of an external examination as a goal means that there is no way in which their achievement can be externally checked. The problem is most acute for those teachers who devote the majority or all of their time-table to the low streams. They have neither the satisfaction of preparing high stream boys for the examinations, nor have they a measure of their own competence and effort through the externally assessed examination results. These teachers of low streams may, like their pupils, feel status deprived. Their motivation to strive must be entirely self-induced. Moreover the unrelenting demands made by low stream, delinquescent pupils on the strength and patience of such teachers must in many cases be almost unbearable. It is hardly surprising that many of them treat their job as a routine, custodial task and thus fail to inspire and motivate their pupils. The result is that they begin to *expect* little of their pupils, who adapt to this reduced expectation with a lowered level of aspiration. This is one of the roots of progressive retardation.[2]

If we are to make full use of the talents of all our teachers it would be wise policy to allocate every teacher to all streams for some part of his time-table. In this way all the teachers can feel that they are sharing both the privilege of teaching the more gifted or motivated children and the burden of educating the more difficult pupils. It may be doubted that the higher stream pupils will suffer in consequence; certainly the low stream boys will gain.

One of the most important results of the segregation of the pupils into streams at Lumley School was, as we saw in Chapter Three, that the boys in one subculture perceive the other subculture as a negative reference group. This does, of course, promote a fear of 'demotion' in high stream boys, but it also tends to undermine the assumptions teachers make about the 'promotion' system in that low stream boys often do not desire, and sometimes actively avoid, promotion into a higher stream. The subcultures are expanded as boys of the appropriate orientation are drawn to the poles. The hostility and lack of communication which exists between the two subcultures is disturbing. The evidence in this research does not offer support to the view that the neighbourhood ('one-class') Comprehensive School will solve many of our educational problems. It may be true that the working class boy is deprived in our middle-class-dominated Grammar Schools, but it is clear that an analogous class warfare is at work in this working class Secondary Modern School.[3]

If these mutually hostile subcultures are to be eliminated – either in a Comprehensive or a Secondary Modern School – the school must provide greater opportunities for members of different streams to interact, preferably in a co-operative enterprise. It would be a comparatively simple task to organize the school time-table in such a way that members of upper and lower streams could take some subjects together, especially in the case of Games, Art, Handicraft, and possibly Music and Religious Education. We saw in Chapter Three that the only point at which the negative stereotypes began to disintegrate was when boys from 4A and 4D were pressured into mutual acceptance and co-operation on the Rugby Team.

Participation in the social life of the school, in such activities as sport, music and school holidays, is at Lumley a reflection of the academic hierarchy of the streams. We have seen how the staff tend to favour the upper stream pupils in the process of selection for these activities. The tendency of the teachers to delete the 'undesirables' from the lists of holiday applicants deprives these boys not only of the holiday and its educational value but also of the opportunity of extended and less formal relationships with teachers which these holidays accord.

On the question of sport most of the teachers believed that it was the boys with superior academic performance – though they often referred to 'ability' – who made the best sportsmen. Whilst it is true that there tends to be a low positive correlation between intelligence and skill at games, the disproportionate representation of high stream boys in sporting activities takes no account of the fact that low stream norms reduce motivation both to achieve academically and to participate in extra-curricular activities, especially when these are associated with loyalty to the school. This means that low stream boys might appear to be less gifted at, and less interested in, sporting activities than is the case. If low stream boys are to take a full share in the extra-curricular life of the school, they must be actively encouraged by the staff to do so.

This point may be illustrated. On one occasion during an

informal discussion with Derek of 4D I learned that he was going to the swimming baths after school. I also discovered that such visits were a regular event for Derek and some of his friends, and that they were fairly able swimmers. When I asked Derek for which events he would enter in the Schools' Swimming Gala, he retorted:

I wouldn't swim for this bloody school.

Derek was also able at Rugby. As previously noted, the master in charge of fourth year Rugby was also the form teacher of 4D, and he was anxious that some of his form members should play on the team. When he met with little response from Derek in trying to persuade him to attend practices, he called the boy 'chicken'. Derek, in his desire to refute this charge of lack of guts, attended the practices and became a regular member of the team. The involvement of low stream boys in such activities is not an easy task for teachers, who will, initially at least, be disappointed by the perfunctory response of such boys. But unless this is done, the development of mutually hostile sub-cultures will tend to persist.

Teaching problems are most concentrated in the low streams. The academically orientated boys in these forms are regarded by the teachers as conformists, whereas on the peer group level they are the deviants; and the 'difficult' boys whom the teacher regards as non-conformists are in fact the high status conformists on the peer group level. This tendency of the teacher to evaluate pupils in terms of his own rather than peer group values has important repercussions. He has little chance of eliciting the desired response from these high informal status but anti-academic boys, because the kinds of reward he offers are considerably inferior to those offered by the delinquescent peer group from which such boys derive their security and status. The result is that when the teacher publicly praises the low status boy for his good work, he is in fact stressing the deviance of such boys from the group norm, and is thus reinforcing the anti-academic norms he seeks to disrupt.

It is possible that more progress could be made if the teachers identified the boys of high informal status and used them as a means of entry to the peer group, for unless the leaders are 'converted' first, there is little hope of effecting any extensive attitude change. When the teacher finds himself locked in permanent combat with the informal leaders, he has forsaken his only chance of directing the behaviour of these boys into the channels he considers desirable. Attempts to compel these boys by force of threat of punishment into an academic orientation are self-defeating and have the reverse effect. It may seem unrealistic to treat 'bad' pupils as if they were 'good' pupils, but if the teacher is to achieve his ends he needs to transform the role conception of the pupils; and to do this he must obtain the loyalty and co-operation of the informal leaders.

One of the writer's former colleagues,[4] an experienced and insightful teacher, seemed to experience little difficulty with the 'awkward' low stream boys. He claimed that the secret of his success was twofold. On taking the form for the first time he would make it quite clear, through words and action, that he 'would have no nonsense'. After asserting his authority, he would take the essential second step, that of identifying and befriending the informal leaders. He would do this by praising them, even when their effort was minimal, and by assigning to them tasks of responsibility which he *expected* them to fulfil. Over a period he was thus able to legitimate both his own authority and his expectations of the pupil role. Once these boys had received favourable recognition from the teacher, the process of re-organization of behaviour and personality around this new role could begin. And the lower status boys would tend to follow their leaders. Such techniques are not panaceas for all teaching problems, but they do indicate that the teacher's manipulation of the informal status hierarchy in difficult forms can have fruitful results.

The most radical way in which the formation of the subcultures could be suppressed at Lumley is through the complete abolition of the streaming system. There is no doubt that the vast majority of teachers in this country regard streaming as basic to the organization of schools[5] and the staff at Lumley were no exception. Only one of the teachers of senior forms was in favour of non-streaming. Some did feel that the introduction of non-streaming would improve the general behaviour level of the school, but they opposed the idea on the grounds that non-streaming would reduce the general level of academic performance. Although some of the less able boys might improve their academic performance, they argued, the progress of the A stream pupils would be restrained. They also believed that it would be impossible, or at least very difficult, to teach a class of boys with a wide variation in intelligence.

The research on streaming is far from conclusive.[6] Some studies claim that pupils in unstreamed schools acquire better social adjustment and more favourable attitudes to school.[7] Daniels found that in unstreamed conditions pupils made gains in I.Q. and in attainment in Arithmetic and English.[8] He has claimed further that streaming slightly lowers the general level of attainment, slightly reduces the attainment of the 'bright' pupils, markedly retards the 'slower' pupils, and artificially increases the range of attainment.[9] Douglas has shown that at each I.Q. level children placed in the upper streams improve their score on his test between the ages of eight and eleven years, whereas those assigned to lower streams show a deterioration in test score during the same period.[10] This is true *within* each social class, even though middle class children are disproportionately represented in the upper streams, as documented by Jackson[11] and others. Thus, despite some non-supportive studies,[12] there is a growing body of evidence which indicates that the streaming system is self-validating in that it to some extent *manufactures* the differences on which it is justified by teachers.[13] This evidence is supported by the claims of many teachers that de-streaming has led to enormous academic and social benefits.[14]

It appears that at Lumley School, and presumably at other similar schools, the development of opposing subcultures is an extreme form of this differentiation process, which is accentuated by, if not actually caused by, the streaming system. The abolition of streaming at Lumley might thus impede the formation of the subcultures and in part the acquisition of delinquent attitudes by low stream boys. Yet if such a policy were adopted, some fundamental re-thinking about teaching methods would have to be made. The supporters of non-streaming have emphasized the need for a committed and convinced staff who want to make non-streaming work and who are prepared to experiment with new teaching methods. A superficial change in the formal organization of the school cannot be expected to create major academic or social changes. At present the staff at Lumley, with one exception, do not believe that de-streaming would contribute to a solution of some of their problems, and this is partly because they do not fully appreciate the far-reaching effects of the streaming system as indicated by this research. Moreover they are convinced that it would be impossible, or at least very difficult, to teach groups of mixed ability.

This belief is based on at least two important assumptions. The first is that their present teaching methods are relatively immutable. The second is their conviction that the forms under a streamed system are indeed homogeneous in terms of ability. In fact the degree of heterogeneity in the fourth year forms was far greater than the teachers realized, for they tended to regard attainment and a positive orientation to the school's values as synonymous with ability. They believed that the A streams contained the 'brightest' boys and the D streams the 'dullest' and from this concluded that over the four years the promotion-demotion transfer system intensified this selection by ability. This is not substantiated by an examination of the I.Q. scores. In terms of I.Q. (from the eleven-plus examination) the homogeneity of the streams had declined, not increased, by the fourth year. The fourth year comprised boys with a range of 42 I.Q. points (71–113). In the A stream the range in I.Q. scores changed from 18 points when the boys were in the second year to 33 points by the fourth year. The equivalent change in the D stream was from a range of 22 to 31 I.Q. points. Alternatively we may say that in the second year the A stream contained 94 per cent of the boys with I.Q. scores above the median, but by the fourth year this figures had declined to 78 per cent.[15]

In a word, the overlap between streams in terms of the I.Q. scores of the boys in this study increased over the four-year period. This is so because membership of a high stream is a function not simply of ability but of positive orientation to academic values, the reverse being true of low streams. It seems that the subcultural formation, especially the development of anti-academic values and the progressive retardation in the low streams, misled the teachers into believing that within the fourth year as a whole there existed a greater variation in ability range than was really the case, and secondly that each stream contained a group that was homogeneous in terms of I.Q. rather than orientation.[16] The teachers' support for the streaming system, and their opposition to non-streaming, thus rests in part on the subcultural divergence which is itself to some extent a product of the streaming system.

It is, of course, impossible to assess the extent to which sub-cultural formation is the direct result of streaming. In this exploratory study we have found that subcultural development is generated by a number of mutually reinforcing factors, of which the organization of pupils into streams is the basic structural component. In other streamed schools these additional factors may or may not be present and there may be further important factors which do not obtain at Lumley. This research cannot be taken as general evidence against streaming, for under different conditions, whether streamed or unstreamed, subcultural development might not take place. In middle class schools, for instance, it may be that there exists a low stream subculture which is far from delinquescent. Yet on the basis of this exploratory study, and on the assumption that Lumley is not atypical of schools in 'problem areas', we would imagine that there are many schools in Britain with similar problems of a similar genesis which may be diagnosed in a similar way. It is the task of future research to examine the distribution and nature of subcultural formation in our schools.

If these research findings are valid for other schools,[17] especially those in 'problem areas', they indicate that major reforms are necessary if their pupils are to be adequately educated and the school is to be a force which draws children away from delinquent values and behaviour. Ultimately the possibility of some reform lies in the hands of the teachers themselves. The *status quo* is based on an elitist view of education, whereby children are educated and socialized to fit into certain preconceived social strata of life in the modern world. If we are to educate all these children to develop and maintain co-operative and satisfying human relation-ships, to lead useful and constructive adult roles in society, to attain a degree of personal integrity and self-realization, many of the assumptions about education we make as parents, teachers, administrators and legislators must be urgently challenged and reformulated.

Appendix I

PARTICIPANT – OBSERVATION
AND ROLE CONFLICT

Participant-observation, like any other research method, is subject to strains and limitations and if we are to evaluate the method, these must be made explicit. The validation of participant-observation is in part a matter of determining wherever possible the reliability of the material obtained. The extent to which the participant-observer disturbs the situation he investigates, and the extent of the limitation imposed by accepting a role within that situation, lead not only to the uncovering of information which may be inaccessible by other methods, but also to deficiencies and difficulties which require elucidation. Some of the advantages and disadvantages which have resulted from participant-observation of Lumley Secondary Modern School are implicit in the main text; it is now time to consider these in a more systematic way.

The method of participant-observation leads the investigator to accept a role within the social situation he studies: he participates as a member of the group as well as observing it. In theory, this direct participation in the group life permits an easy entrance into the social situation by reducing the resistance of the group members; decreases the extent to which the investigator disturbs the 'natural' situation; and permits the investigator to experience and observe the group's norms, values, conflicts and pressures, which (over a long period) cannot be hidden from someone playing an in-group role. The fact that I had three years' experience of teaching and that I was to spend a third of my time in the school teaching classes allayed many of the fears teachers felt about my presence in the school. Within the first few days many of the teachers asked me about my previous experience as a teacher and my attitudes towards a number of educational problems – corporal punishment being a favourite test-question. This helped to remove the suspicion that I was some sort of 'spy' from the authorities. If I had been a teacher, the argument seemed to run, and I was going to do some teaching in the school, then surely I must be looking at the school from *their* point of view.

But not all the teachers remained unconcerned about my presence in the school. This was partly a result of the fact that the nature of my work was never adequately explained to the staff prior to my arrival. The question of my going to Lumley was discussed with the Chief Education Officer and the Headmaster. On this occasion the nature of my work was briefly explained and the Headmaster consented to the study. However, when I arrived at the school two days later, I was told by the staff that the Head had simply circulated a brief note to all the teachers, saying that a sociologist from the University would be coming to work in the school for a short period. The staff had no indication of the type of work I intended to do. Had I spoken formally to the staff for a few moments on my first day at the school, much of the misunderstanding and suspicion of which I was soon to become aware would have been avoided. As it was, too many fears and questions remained unexpressed and unanswered. Moreover, many of the staff came to wish me good-bye at the end of the summer term some three weeks later and were surprised to learn that my work had only just begun.

The problems of participant-observation in a school cannot be understood without a brief preliminary discussion of the teacher-role. We may define *role* as an aspect of the total behaviour of a particular actor occupying a particular *status* or position within a social system. The nature of the role is determined not only by the status of the actor but also by his orientation towards the *expectations* of other actors who hold complementary roles within the system. Since role is often used ambiguously by sociologists, we will, wherever necessary, distinguish between *role-performance* and *role-expectations*. Most roles are performed to different actors or groups of actors, who may have differing role-expectations. It is this complement of role-relationships which R. K. Merton has termed the *role-set*. The content or definition of a role thus consists of the sum of the expectations of all members of the role-set, including the actor himself, and which aspects of the role are used in actual role-performance will depend upon the member(s) of the role-set to which the role-performance is directed.

The persons who form the constituents of the teacher's role-set are, amongst others, pupils, colleagues, the Head teacher, parents, Her Majesty's Inspectors. It is, of course, the first two of these to whom the teacher principally directs his role-performance, since pupils and fellow-teachers are the groups with which the teacher is most frequently in face-to-face relationship. The Head teacher, parents and Inspectors assume less significance because on only rare occasions need the role-performance be determined by their expectations. The teacher's situation is a highly autonomous one: most of the time he is 'his own boss' and not subject to the scrutiny of colleagues or superiors. In Merton's term, the role-set is highly 'insulated' from simultaneous observation by various members of the role-set.

Role-conflict is the exposure of an actor to conflicting expectations which cannot be simultaneously fulfilled. This may be due to one member of the role-set having conflicting role-expectations which require simultaneous fulfilment, or to two or more members of the role-set holding role-expectations which conflict with one another. Resolution of the conflict will often take the form of a compromise, involving the sacrifice of part of each conflicting expectation, or the complete abandonment of one expectation. For the teacher, resolution of role-conflict is often a comparatively simple matter, since he rarely has to perform his role simultaneously before different members of the role-set, whose expectations undoubtedly conflict. If a parent complains, the teacher may, if he wishes, present himself to the parent as a charming, friendly and gentle person whose behaviour has been entirely misunderstood by the child, and then return to the classroom as a harsh disciplinarian. The teacher may discuss the aims of education at length with his colleagues or the Head-teacher, but this does not mean that his views will necessarily be put into practice in the ensuing lessons.

When the barriers separating the various components of the role-set break down, a conflict will arise if the role-performance becomes simultaneously observed by two or more members of the role-set with different expectations. For the teacher, an Inspection may be such an event. Often the role-performance will change since now it is directed mainly to the Inspector rather than to the pupils; it is the Inspector's expectations which demand conformity if the teacher is to obtain formal approval as a teacher. If the teacher is a 'good' teacher, he can satisfy the Inspector *and* the pupils by his normal role-performance, but the presence of an Inspector often transforms the role-performance. At the teacher's disposal are a number of devices by which he can mitigate the effects of the conflict and the danger it brings to his effective control of the situation. Thus he may inform the pupils that the Inspector has come to see *them* in order to reduce disciplinary infringements and increase artificially the enthusiasm of the pupils, both of which support a role-performance directed towards the expectations of the Inspector.

One aspect of my participant-observation in the school was to sit at the back of a form during an ordinary lesson. Whereas initially most of the teachers happily ascribed a teacher-role to me on the basis of my past experience and current teaching within the school, to observe them within the confines of their own classrooms involved a disruption of their usual autonomy and upset their ascription of a teacher-role to me. In exceptional circumstances teachers do see their colleagues at work but for most part the assessment any teacher may make of his colleagues' competency depends upon more indirect information, such as examination results, noise from the classroom, attitude of pupils outside the classroom and gossip. As soon as I became an observer of the classroom situation, I could no longer be regarded as a teacher. Instead my role became more that of the Inspector. The insulation of the teacher's role-set ceased. The conflicts between the teacher's self-image, the expectations of the pupils and the expectations of an observer became manifest.

The resolutions of this conflict took several forms. A few teachers reacted with some kind of withdrawal. (No teacher actually refused to allow me to observe his lessons, and in only one case was the lack of co-operation made open.) Whenever I went into a lesson conducted by Mr. H., he made the boys work quietly out of text books, talked in a whisper to boys at his desk so that I could not hear from the back and declined to speak to the class as a whole unless this became unavoidable. On several occasions he was rather rude to me – although it is only fair to point out that his relations with many of the teachers were perfunctory. For some time I did not go into his lessons – and tried to find some common ground and a more personal relationship with him. This was entirely unsuccessful, but the problem was resolved for me when the teacher left at the end of the Autumn Term.

With other teachers, the changes my presence effected and their resolutions to the conflict took more subtle forms. Mr. O. usually set the form some written work and then joined me at the back of the room, where he chatted with me or told me jokes. Some of his stories have been of considerable use to me, but hints to Mr. O., that this was not the reason for my presence in the form were of no avail and later he took to inviting me into his room 'for a chat'. I did not see how I could prevent this occurrence without offending Mr. O. Mr. F. never refused to let me observe but if he could he decided to read a story to the form or directed a lesson in which the boys played a passive and silent role. Mr. L. invariably sent boys to the back of the room with their books for me to examine and comment on, although when I had seen every book several times this practice declined.

Many of the teachers appeared to behave quite naturally and act as if I was not in the room at all, and it is difficult to check on the extent of the changes my presence produced. Sometimes the teachers would themselves indicate the effects of my presence. In the lower streams in particular the boys are caned comparatively frequently, if the conversations over lunch and in the common room are any measure of this. But it was notable how very rarely a teacher caned a boy when I was in the room. One day, as I was leaving the room, Mr. G. said to me, 'They've got a bit noisy, haven't they? I think I'll cane a few when you've gone.'

A further check came from conversations with the boys, who revealed changes which might otherwise have not been at all obvious.

When you're in he tries to act calmly as though he's a little angel and all that.

Did you notice when you were in, Mr. M's. – he called me by my first name? But when you're on the field (games) he calls you by your second name.

They put on a show for you. They put the good act on, smiles and all that, and when you've gone out . . .

Like if Mr. O's getting mad 'cos someone's ripped a book or something, but if you're in he seems to drop it. If you weren't there he'd get real mad.

Initially my presence also caused changes in the boys' behaviour though I am convinced these are of less importance, for once the boys became accustomed to me, they behaved normally.

It depends on the teacher. With Mr. A. and Mr. O. we never muck about anyway. They're strict and we do what they say. But it's different with Mr. L. Like when you came in the other day. (In the middle of an examination.) Before you came in they were all messing about and there was quite a few with cribs out. But they put 'em away as soon as you came in.

We just forget you're there most of the time.

I never know you're there when you're sitting at the back.

This lack of observability to the pupils is no doubt partially responsible for the small changes my presence made on the boys. But my presence at the back of the class was highly visible to the teacher and thus a constant reminder of the intrusion. It is boys from the lower streams who have commented most on the changes, and I suspect that this is because it is in these forms that disciplinary problems become more acute.

Sometimes the teachers went out of their way to tell me how they thought a class ought to be conducted and this came in direct conflict with their actual behaviour as reported to me from other sources Mr. M. gave me a long homily on the necessity of drawing information from the boys rather than pumping it into them, which, he said,

> would be like trying to pour a bucket of water into a sterilised milk-bottle – a little would go in but most of it would end up on the floor.

He proved to be a strong advocate of some progressive methods of education, yet it is certain that Mr. M. used the cane very frequently and on other occasions he expressed opinions which directly contradicted his lecture to me. Such attempts to deceive me resulted from the ascription to me of an Inspector-role. Yet my continued presence in the school, unlike the brief visit of an Inspector, made such attempts at deception detectable.

Through constant participation in the informal social activities of the staff and the consequent initiation and acceptance into the informal relations, cliques and private jokes and quarrels, I could to a large extent shed the Inspector-role. When matters concerning class discipline, for example, were raised in my presence, the teachers and I were able to obtain a degree of mutual identification and I was able to renounce any expertise or authority that are part of the Inspector-role. An index of the increasing cordiality of my relations with the staff was the extent to which I was drawn into the informal activities: playing darts at lunch time, helping with the school concert, going on school holidays, attending staff parties at the end of term and over Christmas. Yet there were problems. Conversations with the staff over lunch or in the staff room were potential sources of conflict. When the conversation took a controversial turn – especially when the subject was education – I tried to keep silent, but my opinion was frequently sought and I was drawn into the conversation, and forced to take sides. On such occasions participation strongly overrides observation, and may well introduce frictions which could undermine the work. But I have come to the conclusion that if I had not participated naturally in the social life of the teachers – that is, be myself where possible – I could never have been integrated into the group and would have taken the risk of social exclusion. Inevitably I was constantly aware that I was working in the school with research aims, so that every event may be significant for the analysis. But I consider that unless I had behaved naturally my presence would have been more disruptive than ever.

Due to their lack of training in social science, many of the teachers did not realize that some of the casual remarks they made to me, or in my presence, presented me with a fuller picture of the social situation as a whole. In an article on participant-observation, Dr. R. J. Frankenberg has written that:

If the observer cannot participate with the knowledge and approval of the people to be studied he should not be there at all. The observer has a positive duty to be open that his intentions are to observe, to report and to publish an account of what he sees . . .

The difficulty is that most of the people being studied could not appreciate that many of the apparently trivial things they said or the confidences they related *are* of social significance. When I behaved naturally to the teachers, they treated me as an individual person, be it as colleague or friend, and appeared to assume, at least for the moment, that I was not a social psychologist studying the school. Yet it was often at such times that the most significant things were said. Inevitably therefore, a certain amount of deception was involved. Dr. Frankenberg's dictum, though highly commendable in theory, over-simplifies the practical situation. In light conversation with a teacher one cannot suddenly point out that what he has just stated is sociologic-ally important, for this would seriously inhibit future relations. If the observer really does have 'a positive duty to be open in his intentions' then he must constantly remind the people he observes of this fact, whereas in reality they adjust to the researcher's presence and cease, in part, to treat him as such.

This mutual personal adjustment of observer and subjects revealed itself not only in improved personal relationships, but also in the gossip that was related to the observer. I am convinced that many of the stories recounted to me would not have been told at all had I reminded the teacher that I was observing the school. The personal relationship that I established with a teacher led him to say more than he perhaps originally intended and certainly more than he would consider fit for the ears of an observer, though it must be admitted that stories detrimental to the teacher's own colleagues might still be related, since motives for spreading gossip are complex.

The ethical issues raised by these problems are incapable of simple resolution. I do not think that the difficulties encountered make it necessary to rule out all forms of participant-observation as unethical. The moral question is one of the uses made of the material so obtained. Everything one learns in a participant-observer situation assists in the analysis, but the researcher has a duty to use only non-confidential evidence in a published report, and this may mean that there are some aspects of the situation which cannot be published at all because all the evidence must be regarded as confidential information. My information on teacher–teacher relations falls into this category.

Interdependence is a characteristic of most face-to-face groups: the members rely on each other for co-operation and mutual aid and obligation. Through being integrated into the teacher group, I had inevitably acquired ties and obligations. On a number of occasions my own unusual role caused me to be 'used' by the teachers. Whenever I observed a teacher's class, I placed myself under an obligation to that teacher. And some teachers tried to make full use of this obligation. Mr. M. discovered that I sometimes used a typewriter in school and I was soon requested to do some typing for him. Mr. O. asked me to look after his class on a number of occasions. Once, when he wished to attend a meeting of teachers outside school but during school hours, the Headmaster would not allow him to leave the school since there was no teacher available to take care of his class. Mr. O. suggested that I could do it, but the Head pointed out that I was not really on the staff, and certainly not paid by the Authority, so I could not be asked. (I did not learn of this until the following morning.) Mr. M. twice asked me about the discipline of other teachers, which he could not observe directly himself. Mr. G. once used me as an incentive to get the boys to do some written work well. He told them – without consulting me – that I wanted to inspect the work later. At break he asked me if I would go round the form and look at each boy's work. My obligations to him prevented my desire to decline, although I implied that this was not a situation I enjoyed. I may add that many of these boys told me later that they were very dubious about the teacher's claim that I wanted to see their work. This incident was unfortunate. Whereas I was trying to divest myself of a teacher-role with respect to the boys (see below), Mr. G. by asking me to inspect the boys' work, was assigning to me, in the eyes of the boys, the very role I wished to avoid.

By the end of the first term, the Inspector-role assigned to me originally was beginning to fade, and was replaced more fully by a teacher-role. This was partly due to my integration into the informal staff relations and partly due to my taking over some duties of a teacher who was suddenly taken ill. An anecdote may illustrate this. At the end of the Autumn Term the school presented a concert. The first and second years saw this concert on one afternoon and on the following day the audience consisted of the third and fourth years. It so happened that not every teacher was able to see the concert, and I waited until the second performance. However, that morning a teacher asked me if I would look after his class whilst he helped with the make-up. I explained that it was rather important for me to see this concert, and he was very offended when I said that I could not agree to his request. He did not appear to understand that I needed to observe the concert as part of my job. He was treating me as an ordinary member of staff, not as a social scientist with a special function in the school.

Appendix I

Once one acquires a teacher-role, there is a potential conflict over professional jealousies. Dave in 4D was regarded by almost all the teachers as a difficult boy; lazy, loudmouthed, and a trouble-maker. I was teaching him at the time, and in the term test he obtained a high mark and came near the top of the class. Mr. L., who did not like this boy, took exception to this and began to refer publicly to this boy as 'Hargreaves' friend'. Moreover, one of the forms I had been teaching returned to Mr. L. at the end of the Term and one of the boys told Mr. L. that he preferred me to him. This was almost certainly because I am a much younger person than Mr. L. and that I had the advantage of still being novel to the boys. Although Mr. L. reported this as a joke, he was very cool to me for some days and on three separate occasions repeated the same story – as a defence mechanism – of how, during the previous year, the boy who was considered to be the worst in school had told him that he was the only teacher the boys respected. Such professional jealousies, however slight, did not make my task any easier.

There seems little doubt that, despite some difficulties, my assumption of a teacher-role whenever possible (and my conscious attempts to minimize the teachers' tendencies to ascribe other roles to me) proved an invaluable aid in consolidating my position amongst the staff of the school. Naturally, they never completely neglected to see me as a social psychologist, but I consider that my assumption of certain elements of the teacher-role reduced the disruptive effects of a more pure psychologist role. Over a period of six months I began to feel as much a part of the system as if I really were a member of the staff and the teachers, in their turn, treated me as a colleague. This betrayed itself in numerous small ways. For example, one morning when I arrived late at the School, a teacher asked me, quite seriously, if the Headmaster had 'told me off'.

Yet the role-conflicts I experienced as a teacher-researcher existed along another dimension – my relationship with the boys. When I first arrived at the school the boys inevitably ascribed some form of teacher-role to me. Any adult (who is not dressed as a workman) appearing in the school must in their eyes have some strong connection with the teaching profession. Although the Headmaster introduced me to them in assembly as 'a new member of staff', I did not undertake any teaching duties for several weeks, and even then for only a third of the normal teaching timetable. They were mostly aware of me as someone who sat at the back of the class and said little. For these reasons the boys seemed to think that I was either an Inspector or a student-teacher. Later, they discovered that I was teaching; I was seen walking around the school with piles of books; I ate separately with the staff at lunch time, and used the staff room. So the Inspector–student roles gave way to a teacher-role. The usual courtesy title of 'sir' was extended to me when the boys spoke to me or wished to attract my attention.

When I began to take lessons, I was faced with the normal problems of a teacher. Some of the classes I taught were junior forms, so discipline was an easy matter. But with the older boys, and especially the lower streams, I needed to control the class carefully if order was to prevail during the lesson. The first few lessons with a new form are always a period of testing for the boys: they use several techniques by which they check how strict a disciplinarian the teacher will be. During the first three weeks at the school I simply observed; and it became clear that the boys in the lower streams tended to react negatively towards the teachers. For this reason I did not wish those boys to identify me too closely with the teachers. In my teaching duties I felt it was important not to invoke the usual teacher sanctions – the cane or sending the boy to the Headmaster – for this would be to align myself very closely with the teachers, and thus create negative feelings towards me. But if my discipline was not reasonably strict then I would have chaos on my hands during each lesson and would lose the *respect* of the boys. In the event I tried to solve the problem by preparing interesting lessons which gave the boys little opportunity to 'play me up'. Unfortunately this attempt to avoid the necessity of using disciplinary sanctions lasted but a few weeks.

Simultaneously, I was trying to get to know the boys in an informal way. At Lumley this was particularly difficult to achieve. Many of the usual avenues of access to the boys were closed to me. During the short breaks in the middle of morning and afternoon school, the boys were sent out into a small playground. Two teachers were on duty in case of trouble. Often, therefore, I was forced to spend as much time talking to the teachers as to the boys during these ten minute breaks. Moreover, the boys in the lower streams with whom I particularly wished to chat informally usually went to the far corner of the yard where they could smoke in a small alcove. From time to time several boys were caught and caned: but the alcove became their sanctum. I was unable to venture into the alcove, for if boys were smoking and another teacher appeared on the scene I would appear to be condoning the smoking. But if I expected the boys to put out the cigarettes on my arrival, I would be aligning myself with the teachers.

At lunch time the staff ate separately from the boys. After lunch only a few small boys remained in the playground for the rest of the lunch hour. The school had no formal societies, with the exception of a brass band, so I was unable to meet boys informally during such activities. There was no games field near the school: the boys travelled

by bus to a field several miles away. But the boys used the bus as a
changing room. Holidays, school trips and clubs outside the school
provided the only means of making extended informal relationships
with the pupils.

During the first term I felt that my relations with the higher streams
developed well: but with the lower streams a rapid deterioration was
evident. Whenever possible I explained the nature of my work to the
boys who almost invariably showed interest and a willingness to co-
operate. But a minority in the lower streams remained immovably
suspicious. For this reason I took the radical step of giving up all my
teaching periods except for two lessons a week with the B stream. This
seemed to be the only way in which I could divest myself of the
teacher-role. From that point my relations with the boys improved to a
remarkable extent, who not unexpectedly passed through a period of
ambivalence. The delinquent group, for example, began shouting out
to me, 'Hello, sir' in a rather cheeky way, which I would immediately
have crushed as a teacher. Once again, they were putting me to the test,
seeing how far they would go before I would try to punish them. When
I failed to respond as they expected, these attempts at provocation
ceased. My relations with Clint were always shallow: he simply did not
trust me. But I was able to make considerable progress after an
incident in the Spring Term. Clint was involved in a fight during the
lunch hour with a boy from a neighbouring Further Education Centre.
A woman who witnessed the fight rushed into school to complain to
the Headmaster. Fortunately, I saw her before she was able to inform
any of the Staff and hurried to the scene where I was able to warn
Clint of the situation. He seemed very grateful and was less cold to me
after this event. With other members of the delinquent group my
relations were more cordial. Several times I was offered various
pieces of stolen property. Two of these boys came to me to discuss
their latest exploits – the theft of a motorcycle and robbery with assault
– and seemed glad to talk about their misdemeanours with an adult
who had no formal power over them and who would not judge them.
Slowly the boys learned that they could trust me. In order to achieve
this trust I often had to depend upon accidents. When they discovered
I would not report them for offences against the school rules which I
had observed, the teacher-role began to diminish, and was replaced
by a new form of respect and trust. One day a boy told me how he had
broken a school rule. Afterwards I assured him that I would not tell
the teachers. 'I know that,' he said, censuring my statement of the
obvious. On another occasion when a boy hid the teacher's cane I was
admitted into the conspiracy with a wink. At times it was difficult
to avoid entering into active collusion with the boys: a convenient

attack of blindness or deafness proved to be invaluable in resolving such problems. Invitations to youth clubs, beat clubs and the billiard hall, which I gladly accepted, tended to cement my relations with the boys, though 'leaks' about such events caused some surprise to the staff.

Within organizations such as schools, factories, hospitals and prisons, a distinction can be made between the 'controllers' (teachers, managers, doctors and warders) and the 'controlled' (pupils, workers, patients, prisoners). Between these two levels yawns the gap of status distinctions, which a participant-observer cannot necessarily bridge. To participate and observe involves to some extent shedding the researcher-role, since participation means accepting in some degree a normal role within the social situation. But to accept such a role, whilst facilitating the process of absorption into the community, entails limitations on material obtained and bias in its interpretation.

As a social psychologist, I was inevitably something of an intruder in the school. It is difficult to define in detail the content of this role, but it is clear that it is a role which is *external* to the system and will thus create suspicions from the participants. By accepting a teacher-role, I was absorbed into the community of the teachers, but this integration was possible only after I had, through the informal personal relationships which developed over time, shed the Inspector-role which resulted from my observation of lessons. The researcher-role would tend to fade naturally because of its low visibility – in contrast to the high visibility of racial difference which might beset anthropological studies. Yet the gap between the teachers and the pupils could not be bridged. Whereas Whyte in 'Street Corner Society' was able to participate as a member of the gang, I could never assume a pupil-role. In the nature of things, I could never stand completely on one side of the teacher/pupil division. When the study was planned it seemed that the assumption of a teacher-role would be the best way in which the participant-observation could be effected, but it was not foreseen that the assumption of a teacher-role, whilst facilitating my relations with the staff, would seriously inhibit my relations with the pupils. A choice had to be made, and I decided to abandon my carefully nurtured teacher-role to improve relationships with the boys. The conflicts with the staff which I expected to result did not arise: mainly, I suspect, because having once held a teacher-role I had become integrated into the community of teachers, and thus the assumption of a more pure researcher-role at a later stage did not arouse the suspicions which could have occurred if such a role had been assumed at the beginning of the study. To the boys, my place within the community was inevitably something of a mystery, but it was a mystery they seemed to accept uncritically. Part-teacher, part psychologist, part friend and ally, they accepted me as an individual who suddenly became part of the system: but to achieve this, I had to abandon the teacher-role in so far as this was possible.

A social scientist is always a person with his own personality, idiosyncracies and faults. One suspects that as a participant-observer he makes more impact on the people he studies as an individual person rather than as a researcher. Most scientists disturb what they observe to some degree, but in the case of the social psychologist or sociologist the extent of this distortion is relatively larger. A different researcher in the same social situation would make a different impact on the people and they would react to him in different ways. No doubt different discoveries would be made, different aspects emphasized, different interpretations elaborated, even though the central analysis might be the same. Yet more important than this is the extent to which the same single researcher can influence the situation by the roles he adopts. In my own case, the history is one of a conscious manipulation of roles to avoid and control conflicts at different levels in the situation at different stages. There is little doubt that a more consistent adoption of roles would have given me a somewhat different perspective of, and insight into, the social system of the school. As social scientists we assume that a common core of material and interpretation would result, especially if this is based on data collected by 'objective' methods which can be treated statistically. Yet the failure to make explicit the limitations and difficulties of participant-observation would be a failure to assess, however unquantitatively, the margin of error incurred by this method of social investigation.

Appendix II
ABSENCE FROM SCHOOL

In the main text some use has been made of the absence rates at Lumley Secondary Modern School, particularly as they are related to stream. We must now consider these in more detail.

We may define absence rate as the total number of absences as a percentage of the total number of possible times present in school. Table II shows that these rates increase as we descend the streams in the fourth year. To what extent is this true of other year-groups in the school? The rates for the first to third year forms, 1963–4, are given in Table A. (The fourth year boys have been excluded since half of them leave after the second term; the academic year 1963–4 has been used since the Headmaster restreamed some year-groups into four instead of five forms during the year 1964–5.) It is clear that the association between stream and absence rate is not confined to the fourth year; it is true of the school as a whole that the higher the stream the lower the absence rate tends to be.

The absence rate changes according to the day of the week. There is a slight decrease from Monday to Tuesday followed by an increase towards the end of the week. Whilst it may be true, at least in part, that the increase in the absence rate reflects an increase in the illness rate, since presence in school exposes the child to infection, it seems likely that this increase contains a truancy rate. This hypothesis is supported by the last section of Table A. If we subtract the absence rate of Tuesday, the lowest in the week, from that of Friday, we find the difference tends to be stream related: the lower the stream, the greater the tendency towards an increase in the absence rate in the latter part of the week.

From analysis of the absence rates at Lumley over a period of years, the writer found that the absence rates between each year-group do not differ sharply. The trend is not towards change between the first and fourth years in the absence rate for the year-group as a whole, but towards a change in the distribution of this rate between the different streams within each year-group. In the first year the absence rates of

the streams tend to be fairly close together; if we use these as a base-
line, we find that by the fourth year the absence rates of the high
streams have declined and those of the low streams have risen. Let us
consider the absence rates of the boys in this study. We shall compare
the average number of days absent in the first two terms of the fourth
year (after which half the boys left school) with the corresponding
figure for the same group of boys when they were in the first year,
irrespective of which stream they were in during their first year. The
4A boys were absent for an average of seven days in their first year and
by the fourth year this has fallen to an average of six days. In the case
of the 4D boys, their first year average of nine days absent has risen
to twenty-three days by the fourth year. This trend may, of course,
mask the trend for high absentees to fall in stream (see Table III), but
it may also reflect the normative structure and associated pattern of
orientation towards school in the different streams.*

The absence rates for the fourth year forms given in Table II do
not tell us how the absences are distributed among the boys in each
form. It is possible that the high absence rates for the low streams are
the result of a few high absentees. The distribution for the fourth

TABLE A

Stream	A	B	C	D	E	All
Absence Rate	5·04	6·57	8·50	12·71	13·83	8·28
Day	Mon.	Tues.	Wed.	Thurs.	Fri.	All
Absence Rate	8·02	7·85	7·92	8·34	9·33	8·28
Stream	A	B	C	D	E	All
Fri.–Tues.	1·22	1·25	0·87	1·82	2·52	1·48

year forms in this study are given in Table B. Whilst it is true that 4D
contains a few high absentees, the *general* pattern of absenteeism is
different from that in 4A.

A final point is the relation between absenteeism and informal status
in the low streams. This must be considered because of the wide range
of absence rates among the boys in these streams. If the boys are

* An excellent discussion of the relations between attendance and intelligence/
achievement, and the 'vicious circle' effect, can be found in Stephen Wiseman,
Education and Environment, Manchester University Press, 1964, pp.27–29 and 164–7.

divided into a matrix of high and low status against high and low absence rates, the significance of the association can be calculated. In fact, high status is associated with low absence rates (Chi-square=4·45, d.f. = 1, P< ·05). Inspection by the writer of the distribution showed that it is the boys of intermediate rather than very low status who have the highest absence rates. This can be explained in terms of our earlier analysis. The high status boys will have better than average attendance rates, since they derive their status-satisfaction from being in the group, for which they must attend school. The very low status boys who are academically orientated will also have better than average attendance rates, since they must come to school to make academic progress. It is the boys of intermediate to low status who will have the highest absence rates since they are unable to derive full satisfaction from participation in either the high status 'delinquent' group or the low status 'academic' group. There remains little to attract them to school. This hypothesis cannot be adequately supported on the data from this study, but it is hoped that future research might throw further light on the relation between informal status and absence from school.

TABLE B

Days Absent (Autumn and Spring only)	4A	4B	4C	4D
0	7	6	—	1
1–5	15	10	6	2
6–10	2	3	3	2
11–15	2	5	5	4
16–20	2	1	2	—
21–30	—	3	4	6
31–40	2	—	1	3
41–50	—	—	1	2
51–	—	—	—	2

Appendix III

LIST OF QUESTIONS ASKED

1. I want you to write down the names of the boys you go around with most while you are in school. You may write down 1, 2, 3, 4 or 5 names but do not write down more than 5 names. If you mainly go around with just one or two boys, then simply write down those two names. In each case put the form against the name. You may choose the boys from any form in this school.

2. In a form as big as this one, not every boy likes every other boy as much. You like some boys more than others. There may be some boys that you dislike. So write down the names of one or two, but not more than two, boys that you particularly dislike. If you don't particularly dislike any boy, then simply draw a line in the space.

3. Which boy in the whole fourth year do you dislike most? It doesn't matter if it is the same as the one you put in question 2 and it doesn't matter if it is a different name. If you don't dislike any boy in the fourth year, leave a blank.

4. This time I want you to write down the name of your best friend. If he is at this school, write down the name of his form as well. If he is at another school, write down the name of the school he goes to. If he is working, just write 'working' by the side of the name. Remember, this is the one boy who is your best friend.

5. Do you like school or do you dislike school *on the whole*?

6. If you could leave school at the end of this Autumn Term would you do so? Write yes or no.

7. On this page there are three boxes. Next to them is a list of all the boys in this form. You are going to put every boy's name into one of the boxes.

   In the top box write the names of all the boys who are the leaders among the boys in this class. By leaders is meant the boys who take the lead, who run things in the class, the ones the others look up to and follow.

   In the bottom box write down the names of the boys that the lads don't pay much attention to, the lads who are ignored, who are unpopular, who get teased, who never take the lead in things and don't follow what the rest do.

In the middle box, write the names of the boys who don't fit into the other two boxes.

Remember, the question is not asking whether or not you *like* the boys. It is just about the leaders, whether you happen to like them or not.

8. *The Sentence Completion Test*
   (a) All schoolboys should . . .
   (b) When lessons are boring I . . .
   (c) Teachers are . . .
   (d) Teachers here think of me as . . .
   (e) When the teacher tells me my work is bad I . . .
   (f) Boys in 4A are . . .
   (g) Boys in 4D are . . .

9. After you leave this school do you intend to take any kind of further school or night school to continue your studies?

10. *Orientation Test Items*
    (a) I like a boy who has an interesting hobby.
    (b) I like a boy who always comes to school unless he is ill.
    (c) I like a boy who does not pay attention in class.
    (d) I like a boy who plays some game for the school.
    (e) I like a boy who is cheeky to the teachers.
    (f) I like a boy who is clean and tidy.
    (g) I like a boy you can have a lot of fun with in lessons.
    (h) I like a boy who lets you copy his work.
    (i) I like a boy who smokes.
    (j) I like a boy who gets on with his work.
    (k) I like a boy who is always willing to help the teachers.
    (l) I like a boy who has long hair.
    (m) I like a boy who obeys the teachers.
    (n) I like a boy who respects the school.
    (o) I like a boy who is a good fighter.
    (p) I like a boy who comes to school late.
    (q) I like a boy who has good manners.
    (r) I like a teacher who keeps the class quiet and under control.
    (s) I like a teacher who does not punish messers.
    (t) I like a teacher who makes you work hard.
    (u) Boys should be made to wear a school-uniform.
    (v) Boys should be allowed to leave school when they are 14 years old.
    (w) Boys should be allowed to smoke in school.
    (x) Boys should be allowed to wear jeans in school if they want to.

(y) Boys should be allowed to have long hair if they want to.

Other items

  i. I like a boy who is a prefect.

  ii. I like a boy who is not a teacher's pet.

  iii. I like a boy who comes from a good home.

  iv. I like a teacher who is interested in pop music.

  v. I like a teacher who is interested in games.

Lie Check Items

  vi. I like a boy who has a good sense of humour.

  vii. I like a boy who shares things with you.

  viii. I like a teacher who can take a joke and have a laugh with the lads.

  ix. I like a teacher who is friendly with the lads and talks to them.

  x. I like a teacher who tells you interesting stories.

11. It's important to me to get an office job or a skilled job when I leave school. Yes/No.

12. Planning for the future is a waste of time. I agree/I disagree.

13. *Parental Attitude Items*

  i. My parents would like me to have

    (a) a better job than my father's.

    (b) a similar job to my father's.

    (c) do not mind which job I choose.

  ii. My parents

    (a) sometimes discourage me from going around with certain boys.

    (b) don't mind which friends I choose.

    (c) like to know who my friends are but don't mind who they are.

  iii. If I ever came bottom of the form, my parents would

    (*a*) not mind at all.

    (b) be very angry and expect better results next term.

    (c) be a bit sad and tell me to try harder.

  iv. My parents

    (a) allow me to smoke if I want to, but advise me against it.

    (b) don't mind whether or not I smoke.

    (c) will not allow me to smoke.

  v. When I am getting some new clothes

    (a) My parents give me the money and I buy them on my own.

    (b) My parents and I go together, but I choose the style.

    (c) My parents buy them and don't ask for my choice.

  vi. Do your parents expect you to do jobs around the house?

    (a) I do jobs regularly – several times a week.

    (b) I do jobs occasionally – not every week.

(c) I do jobs very rarely.

vii. How often do you go out with your parents, say to see a film or visit a friend or relative?

(a) At least once a month.

(b) Occasionally.

(c) Only rarely or never.

viii. If I arrived home after 11 o'clock at night without having warned my parents, they would

(a) be very angry and punish me.

(b) not mind at all.

(c) tell me off and warn me not to do it again.

ADDITIONAL NOTES

Chapter One

1. Lumley may be regarded as one of the 'problem areas', which are defined by the Newson Report as the old and overcrowded urban and industrial areas where social problems are concentrated. Just under a fifth of the children in the Newsom sample come from such areas. *Half our Future*, A Report of the Central Advisory Council for Education (England), H.M.S.O., 1963, Paragraph 31, p. 10.

2. The boys in 4E were taught for most of the week by their own form teacher. They tended to have little opportunity for interaction with boys from other streams, who regarded them as 'the backward boys'. Most of them remained in the E stream for the whole of their four year career at Lumley (Table XLV). The reader should note the high frequency of a disturbed home background in these boys (Table XXIX). Although there is no observation or interview material on these boys, a regrettable and important loss to the study, data which were obtained from school records on the E streams have been included in the relevant Tables.

3. It is true that the previous year three boys had remained at school for a fith year to enter for the General Certificate of Education, but this was not favoured by most of the teachers.

Chapter Two

1. J. L. Moreno, *Who Shall Survive?* Nervous and Mental Diseases Publishing Co., Washington, D.C., 1934. More recent accounts of sociometric work may be found in J. L. Moreno (Editor), *The Sociometry Reader*, The Free Press, Glencoe, Illinois, 1960, and in K. M. Evans, *Sociometry and Education*, Routledge and Kegan Paul, 1962.

2. This proposition that the higher the rank of a person within a group, the more he will conform to the norms of the group is supported by many studies and is one of the basic hypotheses of George C. Homans in his important work, *The Human Group*, Routledge and Kegan Paul, 1951. Homans goes on to point out that it is also true that in certain respects the higher a man's status in the group, the less he needs to conform to its norms and the less powerful its sanctions against his deviation. These same two points are also made by M. and

C. W. Sherif, *Reference Groups*, Harper and Row, New York, 1964, p. 179. The relation between conformity and deviation for high status members is complex. The leader must on occasions deviate if he is to be the means by which the group can adapt to changes in the external environment. The leader may also deviate in that he may instigate new trends within the group. Such innovation is a form of deviance.

3. Those names in the 'leader' category received three marks; those in the 'ignored' category, one mark; and those in the central residual category, two marks. The total score for each boy was then calculated and ranked. When two boys received the same total score, the boy with the higher number of points in the 'leader' category was assigned to the higher rank.

4. Sociometric studies largely regard status in popularity or personal preference terms. In this research the informal status hierarchy is more concerned to measure, in a crude way, social power or influence, which is defined by R. Lippitt, N. Polansky and S. Rosen, 'The Dynamics of Power', *Human Relations*, Volume 5, 1952, pp. 37–64, as 'the potentiality for inducting forces in other persons toward acting or changing in a given direction'. In this they follow the suggestions of Leon Festinger and Kurt Lewin. Power and popularity usually correlate positively, though some of the conditions under which this fails are suggested by G. A. Theodorson, 'The Relationship between Leadership and Popularity Roles in Small Groups', *American Sociological Review*, Volume 22, 1957, pp. 58–67. Status and popularity have been distinguished by many social psychologists. See, for example, C. A. Gibb, 'The Sociometry of Leadership in Temporary Groups', *Sociometry*, Volume 13, 1950, pp. 226–243; P. E. Slater, 'Role Differentiation in Small Groups', *American Sociological Review*, Volume 20, 1955, pp. 300–16; and M. and C. W. Sherif, op. cit., pp. 140 and 158.

5. This test was administered just before the end of the Christmas Term 1964. It would be useful to know in detail the extent of changes in friendship choices during the course of the year. However, the writer did not wish to burden the boys with too many questionnaires and so did not retest at a later stage in the year. From observation and interview material there seemed to be few changes in this respect, but significant ones are mentioned at the appropriate places in the text.

6. This is not to say that all the 4A boys regarded academic work as inherently valuable. Most of the thirteen boys who remained at school for a fifth year did so on the grounds that the national recognition of the C.S.E. would help them to obtain a better job than would otherwise be possible. Yet there were signs of a much more pro-academic attitude in 4A. As a form they were proud of the fact that the teachers would leave them to continue their work unsupervised. Moreover,

some of the higher status boys would produce homework voluntarily when none was required by the teachers.
7. See Appendix II.

Chapter Three
1. The Newsom Report points out that it is the less able pupils who have the highest absence rates, and often without adequate excuse. They suggest that frequent absence from school and the lack of extra practice which the 'brighter' pupils get through homework may help to make the weaker pupil weaker still. Op. cit., Paragraph 35, p. 11. In our discussion (in later chapters) of the progressive retardation of the low stream pupils, we shall suggest that there are many more contributory factors at work here.
2. The assumption is that group norms express themselves in the internalized attitudes of members, and that these attitudes can be measured. M. and C. W. Sherif, op. cit., p. 165 also suggest that group norms, assimilated by the member, are reflected in attitudinal reaction.
3. See Chapter Two, Note 2.
4. The higher sociometric acceptance of delinquents and truants in low streams has also been demonstrated by I. J. Croft and T. G. Grygier in 'The Social Relationships of Truants and Juvenile Delinquents', *Human Relations*, Volume 9, 1956, pp. 439–63. They also found significant negative correlations between teacher ratings and sociometric status in low streams.

Chapter Five
1. J. B. Mays, *Education and the Urban Child*, Liverpool University Press, 1962, p. 180.
2. These figures are derived from the table in Paragraph 60 of the Newsom Report, op. cit., p. 23.
3. Some of the teachers exerted informal pressure on pupils to remain at school for a fifth year, though their efforts met with little success.
4. A similar point is made by John Partridge in his study, *Middle School*, Gollancz, 1966, p. 82.
5. The form teacher of 3B, an enthusiastic, able and progressive young teacher, encouraged 3B boys to emulate 3A boys. He, too, was anxious to imbue his pupils with a strong corporate spirit and a sense of achievement.
6. With this hostility shown by low stream boys towards their teachers was mingled a kind of affection. It is perhaps that these boys rejected the teacher's attempt to impose academic standards upon them, not the man himself. They realized that the low stream teachers tolerated

or ignored much behaviour for which the boys could justifiably have been punished.

7. This discussion is indebted to the ideas developed by Erving Goffman in his book, *The Presentation of Self in Everyday Life*, Doubleday Anchor Books, New York, 1959.

8. Parsons breaks down the characterization of the pupil into two components: the cognitive (i.e. academic achievement) and the moral (i.e. responsible behaviour). Talcott Parsons, 'The School Class as a Social System: Some of Its Functions in American Society', *Harvard Educational Review*, Volume 29, 1959, pp. 297–318, and reprinted in various readers such as *Education, Economy* and *Society*, edited A. H. Halsey, J. Floud, and C. A. Anderson, The Free Press, Glencoe, Illinois, 1961, pp. 434–55.

9. An excellent study of the self-fulfilling prophecy is given by R. K. Merton as Chapter XI of *Social Theory and Social Structure*, The Free Press, Glencoe, Illinois, 1957 (revised and enlarged edition).

Chapter Six

1. At Lumley School members of this 'delinquent group' cannot be sharply distinguished from non-members. For this reason we have preferred the term 'group' to 'gang'.

2. The classic work on delinquent gangs is F. M. Thrasher, *The Gang*, University of Chicago Press, 1927. Many interesting comparisons may be made between the 'delinquent group' and Thrasher's findings.

3. There is little doubt that some of the teachers perceived long hair in boys as a threat to the masculine sex role. It is possible that in this respect they betrayed their own sex role insecurity.

Chapter Seven

1. A chi-square test fails even when the E streams are excluded from the calculation. Many studies – for example, Brian Jackson, *Streaming: an education system in miniature*, Routledge and Kegan Paul, 1964 – have found high positive correlations between social class and stream on the aggregate figures of the distribution in many schools. It is possible that social class selection cannot be demonstrated at Lumley School because the Registrar-General's system of classification is too crude for differentiating among working class children. Evidence of social selection at Lumley is presented later in the chapter. It seems likely that father's occupation is a poor measure of the operation of social selection in schools. In this respect the writings and research of Basil Bernstein have made a notable advance. It is also worth asking whether the claims made for the extent and influence of social class

selection in a *single* school have been exaggerated at the expense of other factors.

2. J. W. B. Douglas, *The Home and the School*, MacGibbon and Kee, 1964.

3. The negative relationship between I.Q. and attainment and family size is also fully documented by S. Wiseman, *Education and Environment*, Manchester University Press, 1964; E. D. Fraser, *Home Environment and the School*, London University Press, 1959; J. Nisbet, 'Family Environment and Intelligence', *Eugenics Review*, Volume 45, 1953, pp. 31–42, reprinted in A. H. Halsey, J. Floud, C. A. Anderson, op. cit., pp. 273–87; J. E. Floud, A. H. Halsey, F. M. Martin, *Social Class and Educational Opportunity*, Heinemann, 1957.

4. The relationship between delinquency and family size and overcrowding are reported in T. Ferguson, *The Young Delinquent in his Social Setting*, Oxford University Press, 1952, pp. 20–21.

5. For example, T. Ferguson, op. cit., p. 24; D. H. Stott, 'Do working mothers' children suffer?', *New Society*, 19 August 1965.

6. J. W. B. Douglas, op. cit., pp. 62–3.

7. E. L. McDill and J. Coleman, 'Family and Peer Influences on College Plans of High School Students', *Sociology of Education*, Volume 38, 1965, pp. 112–26.

8. The Newsom Report states that the children in their study watch television for rather more than two hours a day. Op. cit., Paragraph 216, p. 73.

9. T. Ferguson, op. cit., p. 38f., reports that delinquents tend to visit the cinema more regularly than non-delinquents.

10. The Newsom Report states that nearly half the boys in their study do some part-time paid job. Op. cit., Paragraph 34, p. 11.

Chapter Eight

1. Albert K. Cohen, *Delinquent Boys: The Culture of the Gang*, The Free Press, Glencoe, Illinois, 1955, p. 28.

2. R. K. Merton, op. cit., Chapter IV.

3. This is not to say, of course, that members of the 'delinquent group' did not show considerable resourcefulness, especially in disrupting lessons and in the commission of theft. It is *positively* directed resourcefulness which is intended here.

4. We suggest that this in part explains the widely reported high correlation between delinquency and low academic attainment. T. Ferguson, op. cit., p. 119, found that a low level of attainment was probably the most powerful single factor associated with high incidence of delinquency.

5. T. M. Newcomb, 'Autistic Hostility and Social Reality', *Human Relations*, Volume 1, 1947, pp. 69–86.

6. Willard Waller, in his classic *The Sociology of Teaching* (1932), Science Editions, Wiley and Sons, New York, 1965, p. 335, also points out that when a relationship of hostility exists between the teacher and the student, unfavourable recognition by the teacher acts as a positive identification mechanism.

7. The obsessive concern with masculinity of delinquents is thought by many to be a compulsive reaction formation which is the result of cross-sex primary identifications. See A. K. Cohen, op. cit., W. B. Miller, 'Lower Class Culture as a Generating Milieu of Gang Delinquency', *Journal of Social Issues*, Volume 14, 1958, pp. 5–19; J. McCord, W. McCord and E. Thurber, 'Some Effects of Paternal Absence on Male Children', *Journal of Abnormal and Social Psychology*, Volume 64, 1962, pp. 361–9. We feel that the exaggerated masculine behaviour may be more simply explained in terms of the importance of fighting ability and 'threat displays' for status in the delinquent group, combined with the premature imitation of adult male roles.

8. It is significant that the 'cock of the school' in the previous year smoked a cigarette in the middle of the school playground in open defiance of the teachers on his last afternoon in the school.

9. The importance of the school in the generation of delinquency has been inadequately treated in the literature. Some discussion is devoted to the role of the school in A. K. Cohen, op. cit., and in D. J. Bordua, 'Delinquent Subcultures: Sociological Interpretations of Gang Delinquency', *Annals of the American Academy of Political and Social Science*, Volume 338, 1961, pp. 119–36.

10. A. K. Cohen, op. cit.

11. W. B. Miller, op. cit.

12. In his article in the *Journal of Social Issues*, Volume 14, 1958, pp. 20–37, Cohen accepts that the delinquent, whilst committed to the deviant system, recognizes the moral validity of the dominant normative structure. M. and C. W. Sherif, op. cit., emphasize that youths from *all* social backgrounds are influenced by the American 'success' ideology and desire the same tangible symbols of that success (p. 199). Even boys in lower class areas accurately perceive the value of education for future occupational success (p. 200). They differ from middle class youth only in their lower probability of attaining these goals (p. 219). This restriction of opportunity for lower class boys is central to the thesis of R. A. Cloward and L. E. Ohlin, *Delinquency and Opportunity*, Routledge and Kegan Paul, 1961.

13. A. K. Cohen, op. cit., p. 43.

14. The function of the school in providing the delinquent with a tangible enemy is emphasized by J. Webb, 'The Sociology of a School', *British Journal of Sociology*, Volume 13, 1962, pp. 264–72.

15. When we compare the distribution of responses to these seven items of boys in the A and D streams in the second and fourth years, we find that 4A shows more pro-school responses than 2A in six cases out of seven, and fewer anti-school responses in five cases out of seven. 4D shows fewer pro-school responses than 2D in four cases out of seven, but more anti-school responses in only two cases out of seven. This may indicate that in the third and fourth years at school the A stream makes greater movement towards an academic orientation than does the D stream towards an anti-academic, delinquescent orientation. Such an inference is supported by the fact that 2A and 2D show the same negative correlation of $-\cdot37$ between informal status and behaviour (See Table XLVIII).

16. The earlier development of a delinquescent subculture could be facilitated by primary differentiation in the Junior School. This would be most likely when the Junior School contains several streams, which was not the case in the Junior Schools which 'fed' Lumley Secondary Modern School. Subject to future research findings, we suggest, for reasons to be elaborated in the main text, that the formation of a delinquescent subculture is improbable before adolescence, though the roots may be laid many years before its appearance.

17. As W. Waller, op. cit., p. 179, points out, pupils tend to heroify children who are a few years older than themselves, especially those who are in the next higher age group.

Chapter Nine

1. The literature on the adolescent has now assumed gargantuan proportions. One of the best and most original reviews of the literature is David P. Ausubel, *Theories and Problems of Adolescence*, Grune and Stratton, New York, 1954.

2. Progressive retardation seems to be a function of many inter-related factors, which urgently require investigation. In addition to the organizational variables indicated in this study, we suggest that the following may be important:

(a) the reduction of teacher expectation of academic performance of low stream pupils and the consequent imposition by teachers of excessively easy tasks on such pupils.

(b) the reduction of level of aspiration and the inhibition of performance potential by these pupils due to lack of academic demands and adequate incentives.

A most important work relevant to (a) and (b) is Harry Helson, *Adaptation-Level Theory*, Harper and Row, New York, 1964. Other important experimental studies of the effect of adaptation to the level of difficulty to the task may be found in three articles by A. W. Heim:

'Adaptation to the level of difficulty in intelligence testing', *British Journal of Psychology*, Volume 46, 1955, pp. 211–24; 'Psychological adaptation as a response to variations in difficulty and intensity', *Journal of Genetical Psychology*, Volume 56, 1957, pp. 193–211; 'Adaptation to level of difficulty in judging the familiarity of words', *British Journal of Educational Psychology*, Volume 34, 1964, pp. 109–19; and in C. A. Mace, 'The influence of indirect incentives upon accuracy of skilled movements', *British Journal of Psychology*, Volume 22, 1931, pp. 101–14; and J. Szafran and A. T. Welford, 'On the relation between transfer and difficulty of the initial task', *Quarterly Journal of Experimental Psychology*, Volume 2, 1950, pp. 88–94.

(c) the way in which low stream membership produces a sense of relative failure, leading to an expectation of future failure.

(d) the power of the anti-academic group norms to inhibit level of aspiration, motivation and performance.

On (c) and (d), indications of experimental support may be found in H. H. Anderson and H. F. Brandt, 'Study of motivation involving self-announced goals of fifth grade children and the concept of level of aspiration', *Journal of Social Psychology*, Volume 10, 1939, pp. 209–32; P. S. Sears, 'Level of aspiration of children under conditions of success and failure', *Journal of Abnormal and Social Psychology*, Volume 35, 1940, pp. 498–536; G. Rasmussen and A. Zander, 'Group membership and self-evaluation', *Human Relations*, Volume 7, 1954, pp. 239–51; A. S. Dreyer, 'Aspiration behaviour as influenced by expectation and group comparison', *Human Relations*, Volume 7, 1954, pp. 175–90.

3. D. N. Holly, 'Profiting from a Comprehensive school', *British Journal of Sociology*, Volume 16, 1965, pp. 150–7, shows how a comprehensive school selects by social class in its academic and social life. We feel that even in an exclusively working class comprehensive school subcultural differentiation will take place unless preventive measures are taken. This study thus offers no support to those who claim that if working class children are placed in a separate school, the deleterious effect of middle class children will be removed, leading to a greater involvement of all working class children in the academic and social life of the school. J. S. Coleman, *The Adolescent Society*, The Free Press, Glencoe, Illinois, 1961, shows the formation and orientation of peer-group elites in American High Schools is not a simple function of social class composition. We suggest that discussions of the social class composition of schools often exaggerate the influence of social class at the expense of other variables.

4. Mr. R. G. Lee of Hull Grammar School.

5. J. C. Daniels, 'The effects of streaming in the Primary school' (Part I), *British Journal of Educational Psychology*, Volume 31, 1961, pp. 69–78.

6. A. Yates and D. A. Pidgeon, 'The effects of streaming', *Educational Research*, Volume 2, 1959–60, pp. 65–9.

7. C. J. Willig, 'Some implications of streaming in the Junior school', *Educational Research*, Volume 5, 1962–3, pp. 151–4.

8. J. C. Daniels, 'The effects of streaming in the Primary school' (Part II), *British Journal of Educational Psychology*, Volume 31, 1961, pp. 119–27.

9. J. C. Daniels, 'Research on streaming in the Primary school', *Forum*, Volume 4, No. 3, 1962, pp. 79–84.

10. J. W. B. Douglas, op. cit.

11. B. Jackson, op. cit.

12. A. Yates and D. A. Pidgeon, op. cit. and W. G. A. Rudd, 'The psychological effects of streaming by attainment', *British Journal of Educational Psychology*, Volume 28, 1958, pp. 47–60.

13. E. Blishen, 'Conference on non-streaming', *Forum*, Volume 5, No. 2, 1963, pp. 39–45.

14. W. Pattinson, 'Streaming in schools', *Educational Research*, Volume 5, 1962–3, pp. 229–35; E. Harvey, 'Unstreaming a Junior school', *Forum*, Volume 2, No. 2, 1960, pp. 47–9; P. D. Houghton, 'How I teach an unstreamed class', *Forum*, Volume 3, No. 3, 1961, pp. 101–3; K. Coram, 'An experiment in non-streaming', *Forum*, Volume 4, No. 3, 1962, p. 104–6; E. Triggs and J. E. F. Witham, *Forum*, Volume 5, No. 1, 1963, pp. 29–30; D. Thompson, 'Towards an unstreamed Comprehensive school', *Forum*, Volume 7, No. 3, 1965, pp. 82–9; S. G. Rees, 'Streaming and non-streaming', *Forum*, Volume 7, No. 3, 1965, pp. 80–1.

15. It is true that the reduction in the average I.Q. in the A stream is in part the result of the transfer of B and C stream pupils into the A stream because of their desire to enter for the C.S.E. But this does not account for changes in the D stream, which in the second year contained none of the boys with I.Q. scores above the median, but 6 per cent in the fourth year.

16. Cf. J. Partridge, op. cit. p. 72.

17. Our knowledge of subcultural formation in school rests largely on American research. Classics in this field include: A. B. Hollingshead, *Elmstown's Youth*, Wiley, New York, 1949; C. W. Gordon, *The Social System of the High School*, The Free Press, Glencoe, Illinois, 1957; J. S. Coleman, *The Adolescent Society*, The Free Press, Glencoe, Illinois, 1961.

There is, however, considerable danger in transposing the results of this research to schools in Britain, where similar studies are singularly lacking. A good example of small-scale British work, which is very closely allied to the theoretical approach of this book, is H. J.

Hallworth, 'Sociometric relationships among Grammar school boys and girls between the ages of eleven and sixteen years', *Sociometry*, Volume, 16, 1953, pp. 39-70.

INDEX